Res

By the same author

WHEN WE GROW UP

Response

by

Bahíyyih Na<u>kh</u>javání

GEORGE RONALD
OXFORD

GEORGE RONALD, Publisher
46 High Street, Kidlington, Oxford OX5 2DN

ISBN 0-85398-106-X (cased)
ISBN 0-85398-107-8 (paper)

Printed in the United States of America

Contents

Acknowledgements   vii

Preface   viii

One   The Hidden and the Manifest   1

Spiritual Language
Two Books
Contraries

Two   The Hearing Ear   21

Lamentations and Betrayal
A Perfect Listener
The Mystery of Reversal

Three   Advocacy   36

The Inner Voice
The Unbroken Union

Four   The Power of Utterance   50

A Double-Edged Sword
Two Kinds of Power
The Unsheathed Soul
The Active Force

Five   Bonds   63

The Principle of Integration
Vulnerability
Justice
Ideal Communication
Resolution

Six   Compassion and Consultation   84

Vision and Form
Twin Languages
Compassion and the Individual
Consultation and the Spiritual Assembly

Seven   The Mother Word   103

The Mother Temple
The Inward Eve
The Maiden and the Flower
The King and the Comb
Thus Far and No Farther

Conclusion   121

Bibliography   125

References   127

Acknowledgements

IT IS CUSTOMARY to acknowledge the assistance and encouragement of those who have responded to one's thoughts and enabled one to write a book. But that does not seem enough. I would also like to acknowledge the lack of response, for its absence first compelled me to recognize its necessity, and provided me with examples all round.

However, once conceived, this book owed its very existence to the flow of response from friends and family, without whose advice, assistance and collaboration nothing would have survived. I would express my gratitude, in particular, to David and Marion Hofman who enabled me both to see the value and pursue the refinement of these ideas; to Roger White and Winnifred Harvey who listened subtly enough that I might hear what could be said; to Jane Faily, Elizabeth Rochester and a host of other heroic Bahá'í women who inspired and stimulated many of these thoughts; and above all to my father, 'Alí Nakhjavání, whose example and encouragement will always teach me about the wonder and humility that await the soul who responds with a full heart to this Cause and who receives a portion from the wealth of words it offers to mankind.

Preface

WHENEVER ONE LIGHT is added to another in a darkened place we see more and further than we did before. Whenever the words of God are placed in juxtaposition with each other we find that their combined rays light up the shadows in our minds; we see beyond the obscurity of our limitations and glimpse the purpose of our lives. For the words of the Báb, Bahá'u'lláh, and 'Abdu'l-Bahá, like spots of light from a single source, reveal a unified radiance interlinked by infinite rays. And when we let the light of these words work upon us, we discover intricate filaments and interrelationships between apparent contraries that reflect how vast in scope and subtle in design is the Revelation of Bahá'u'lláh.

This book will attempt to bring together a variety of statements from the Writings of the three Central Figures of the Bahá'í Faith – the Báb, its Herald, Bahá'u'lláh, its Founder, 'Abdu'l-Bahá, its Perfect Exemplar – and of its Guardian, Shoghi Effendi, all of which illumine certain connections between apparently dissimilar ideas, and which consequently indicate relationships between aspects of the world around and within us that would not at first sight appear to have much in common. For it would seem that the unique claim of the Bahá'í Revelation does not lie in its definition of dichotomies, or in the challenge to which it calls mankind to resolve these dichotomies through a lifetime of faith and deeds. Instead it would seem that the fundamental premise of the Bahá'í Faith is that integration and resolution are at work all the time around us, and that our perception of dichotomies or contraries is the result of a partial vision which at best shows us a fragment of the mighty patterns at work in the universe.

In order to illustrate this truth I have chosen brief details from the lives of three significant women: Bahá'iyyih <u>Kh</u>ánum, titled the Greatest Holy Leaf, who was the sister of 'Abdu'l-Bahá; Navváb, who was the wife of Bahá'u'lláh and called His consort in all the realms of God; and finally Ṭáhirih, the impetuous heroine and pure-tongued poet of the Bábí Dispensation. Since the role of women, their identity and perception of purpose have so radically changed as a consequence of the revolutionizing spirit of this Revelation, it fascinated me to see how the mysterious words of God worked their wonder on the lives of these three women in order to bring about a reconciliation between the traditional roles of the sexes, a dichotomy that has dominated our thinking for centuries.

This reconciliation can only be effected by a complementary process at work between contraries, a process which I have defined for the purposes of this book as *response*. The reason I have chosen to illustrate the Bahá'í principle of integration through the metaphor of men and women is because the high station afforded to women by Bahá'u'lláh casts an extraordinary light of importance upon the concept of response. Furthermore, I have chosen the metaphor of the tongue and ear to explore this concept of response because the reader of the Bahá'í Writings, who is searching for a resolution between contraries, will find that by so doing he is learning a new language based on spiritual sounds and syllables which enables him to decipher the harmonies within himself and the world. Finally, it is the curious interaction between these two metaphors, that of men and women, and tongue and ear, which I believe may broaden our understanding of the relationship between the soul and its Creator, and quicken the hearts with a glimpse of the infinite nature of this Cause.

This book will have achieved its highest expectations if it can convey to the reader my personal wonder in this limited reading of the Writings, and its greatest aim is to offer these precious Writings in a manner that does not detract from the reader's own variety of wonder. For discovery is an infinite and eternal process, and the luminous nature of the Writings lends us a perpetual and fresh source of light that cannot be dimmed, however limited our response to it might be.

CHAPTER ONE

The Hidden and the Manifest

THERE IS a story from the Bushmen of South Africa about a man who had a herd of cows. Each day he left them in the open pasture and each night they came home rich with milk. One day he noticed with alarm that they were coming home quite drained, and so he hid himself in the bushes, determined to catch the thief. The cows grazed contentedly, and as the evening star rose in the sky, the farmer saw a strange sight. A white rope tumbled out of the clouds and, quick as gossamer, the sky-maidens descended, settled down immediately, and drank the full day's milk. The farmer roared out of the bushes in a fury, but the maidens were too quick for him. Fleet as fantasy they fled up the rope and disappeared, except the last, whom the farmer seized by her fair wrist and held fast. As he raised his knife to stab her, his eyes fell full on her face – and she was beautiful. So he loved her instantly, and she became his wife.

Long and mellow were their years of marriage and the farmer was content although he never knew much about his maiden. She cherished him with gentleness and shared with him his troubles and his joys, and so he was in para-

dise, until one small thing began to spoil his ease. At her
belt the sky-maiden always carried a small straw basket,
which she laid beside her pillow every night. This, she said,
contained the secrets of the sky which might never be lost,
and so her husband did not touch it. One night, however,
his curiosity overcame him:

'Why does my wife keep secrets from me?' he thought. 'I
must see what she keeps inside this basket . . . ' and,
waiting for her to fall asleep, he opened the basket and
looked inside.

When she awoke the next morning the sky-maiden
heard a mocking voice: 'So! You tried to fool me, did you?'
said her husband. 'For all these years you have been giving
me this nonsense about secrets from the sky! Why, the
basket's empty!'

'Empty?' she repeated, looking at him strangely.

'Yes, empty!' he retorted with a scornful laugh. 'There's
nothing in it at all!'

'Nothing?' she echoed, and her voice was as frail as the
breeze at dawn. And turning from him disappointed, she
began to walk away. He called to her, but found he had
forgot her name. He ran to reach her, but she passed and
vanished like a cloud on the horizon. All through his life he
stumbled after her, but the sky-maiden was never found
by him again.

We belong to a generation of vanished sky-maidens. We
feel unnourished though we own whole herds of cattle.
Our baskets of ideals have been proven empty time and
again, and walking the city streets we see strange separations between eyes and smile. Perhaps we have become
such conscientious farmers that we are in danger of becoming positively bovine; a farmer cannot survive by cud
alone.

This story is about a divorce that has uprooted more than marriage in the world. It is about the result of separation between mind and heart, body and spirit, reason and insight. It tells of a scattering in society and within the psyche, of a division between races and temperaments, methods and motives, whose elements now war across our lives.

And yet, as the story suggests, although we have sustained such loss, we long to reconcile the contrary elements within us, symbolized here by the farmer and the maiden. We yearn to heal the breach between them. We hunger for a harmony between polarities in our lives, for without it we hazard all we have. Our world is plagued by polarities, of east and west, of black and white, of male and female, and, far from providing us with the healthy tensions of progress, they have begun to tear us apart.

As a result of this divorce, we have split language too. We have one language for cows, bank accounts and politics, and quite another for dreams, love and mysticism. The latter refers to the former as insignificant and shallow; the former believes the latter to be ephemeral and valueless. The divorce between these two languages not only keeps us ignorant of ourselves but undermines our understanding of their complementary natures. For when the farmer/materialist in us is unaware of the contents of the basket he is a prey to superstition, and when he persists in assessing these contents with his vegetable eyes, he sees nothing. In both instances he is deprived of true knowledge for he has been unable to admit the interdependence of these contrary languages, and so becomes an exile in a world of psychological loneliness that is deeply familiar to our society.

It might be timely, then, for us to reassess the contents of

the basket in a language that is universal and might heal
the breach between body and soul, mind and heart. It
might be possible for our generation, who have become
such experts at divorce, to distinguish now between real
marriage and its limitation, true resolution and its substitute. The oneness between the farmer's fields and the
meadows of the sky can only be conveyed in a language at
once vast and intimate: not one which dilutes their
differences but one which casts broad highways of sweet
light between the two. The response between the farmer
and the maiden within us requires a pattern of communication at once practical and profound: one that is
based neither on suppression of knowledge nor on ma-
nipulation of power, but is conditioned by the dependence
of one contrary on the other. We need a language that at
once admits the limitations of our basket/minds and
simultaneously recognizes the similarities between their
contents and the broad fields above us.

Although we are acquainted with the language of protest, the songs of pain, the poetry of perversity, we find
these do not quite convey the contents of the basket. As
subtle as we may try to sound, our psychological interpretations also leave us less than satisfied. Indeed, whatever
contemporary language we employ to fill the basket with
socio-sexual-political jargon, there is still the separation to
contend with that makes us crave a more comprehensive
resolution. And so, in spite of being tossed by elements of
choice and impotence, we sense amidst this chaos that a
deeper language waits to be articulated. Listening with an
ear tuned to receive these universal harmonies we lean to
hear what secrets whisper in us, undefined, unnamed. And
responding to the One through Whose Will all contraries
were formed, we may begin to conceive of the real re-

sponse between the forces that jostle in our lives.

Spiritual Language

For Bahá'ís the nature of the Covenant between God and man is the crystallization of all we mean by response. The breakdown in that essential communication creates the alienation and loneliness we feel in a society where there is no commitment to an ideal. Ignorance of its need is indicated by the psychological distress within an individual who cannot reconcile his material and spiritual powers. The Covenant affects every fibre of our lives and vibrates through the pulse of our relationships with others. It forges bonds between our hearts and loosens our chained minds to dance in universal harmonies. It is the music and the language implicit in the sky-maiden's basket and the story does not underestimate our ignorance nor our curiosity to know more about it.

This encircling power of the Covenant speaks a language of totality that is not easy to convey in conventional forms, although it is a concept that sets our minds in motion. If possible this book should have been written in a circle, but it is not easy to give even a single thought, full, sweet and spherical, from one mind to another. We usually cut the peach in segments and share it piece by piece. We could, of course, be arch and clever and invite a reader to dance backwards through chapters in order to make sense of a book, but by and large we plod forwards, or think we do. Training and expectation demand that we stay sensibly on the straight lines of syntax and proceed with recognizable gestures of progress along the path or road or highway of a rational argument. The patrol police are on the lookout for an anti-social verb, a stray phrase of adverbial discontent, a herd of semi-colons that confuse the on-coming traffic. The sirens of grammatical decorum pull us up sharp. If we would not be fined for folly we must stop.

But something in the soul tugs, pulls and begs to be set free. Anticipating ends in the beginning, it appeals for release from the steady pulse of sentences and paragraphs. It circles round a thought oblivious of punctuation; it refuses resolution of a single verb. Conceived in galaxies of the imagination, it searches for suns in the atoms of a preposition, and hungers for a glimpse of wholeness in a single noun. It leans out of the windows of verbal progress to see beyond this order to some vaster one.

So, though we use language, we would leap beyond its confines. Though inmates of a world of time and space, and broken-winged, the soul would leap this slow contingent place and, using all the tools that it can find, would sing its way out through the verbs and nouns. It seizes all it can – ear, tongue, power and sex – for it must somehow solve the paradox of symbol and of syntax. These instruments of the groping mind find their way blindly, inch by inch, across the blotted pages of our history, while the articulate soul beats at the bars of their illiteracy and briefly spells itself in poems, pictures and in songs. When will we let it loose upon our simple tongues and hear its beauty? When will we lean the inner ear towards those harmonies that fill the universe about with echoing response?

Myriads of mystic tongues find utterance in one speech, and myriads of hidden mysteries are revealed in a single melody; yet, alas, there is no ear to hear, nor heart to understand.[1]

There is a language lying all about us that we have not

learned to read. There is a syntax of the spirit that we hunger for. But, accustomed to the arrow roads of grey assumption and the fierce possessive drive for resolution, it is hard for us, this desperate generation, to turn aside from the highway, to hear the cry of the untouched corn behind the hedgerows, greet the kernelled wheat that lies like a benediction round us, and consider what we've missed. All that the blizzard and the sun in turn have kissed, our very souls unpeopled by this haste, we toss like cigarette ash from the window, and the journey's passed. The road, its teeth clenched in grammatical assertion, has forgotten what it chased. Something that's contrary to suicide is lost.

But somehow, in spite of time and space and adjectives, we have begun to wander through the soul's vast land. Through centuries of detour and distraction we have at last begun to learn the principles of reading in a spiritual sense. We have been taught to press our fingers on the inner pulse and know what makes the heart grow happy and the thoughts grow sad. We are gradually discovering the quiet knowledge of the mindless speed we had. And it has cost us many casualties along the way, for headstrong children with a high potential for excellence are often the most difficult to teach, and we have abused our Teachers appallingly. Yet with patience They returned, and with persistence They repeated what we long ago had heard: that we should love, that we could learn of love through obedience, that our obedience to the will of God extended our capacities to love each other, to see the relationships between each other, to recognize the tokens of His love amongst us.

The prophets and messengers of God have been telling us, in simple lessons of this kind, that interrelationships between men and God constitute the purpose of existence on this planet. They have repeated the lesson in so many different forms, drawn our attention to so many different levels of harmony, taught us, syllable by syllable, the ethical principles of divine grammar at work in creation, that we might at last stand at the threshold of literacy, see the spiritual connections between apparent contraries, submit our individual sounds to the greater laws of His pronunciation, and read.

It has been in order to teach us this art that the Manifestations of God have been gradually training the distracted child of humanity from age to age, so that our civilizations might progressively advance, and we might be able to develop faculties to decipher the great book of creation around us. Bahá'u'lláh, like the great Teachers before Him, draws our attention again to a resonance beyond the immediate sensory perceptions about us, and recalls for us those irrefutable laws of spiritual literacy without which the conduct of human life on this planet would produce nothing but cacophony:

O My Friends! Have ye forgotten that true and radiant morn, when in those hallowed and blessed surroundings ye were all gathered in My presence beneath the shade of the tree of life, which is planted in the all-glorious paradise?[2]

The principles of reading were few and simple, and using them we might by now have seen and heard all that has been intended for us:

O Friends! Prefer not your own will to Mine, never desire that which I have not desired for you, and approach Me not with lifeless hearts, defiled with worldly desires and cravings.[2]

To perceive creation as an expression of God's Will, to incline ourselves with unconditional responsiveness to what He wills, and to receive the impact of that Will with all the vivid fervour of our consciousness, is something like a lesson in how to read. For unless we turn whole-heartedly to His words, and listen to them without fear or doubt, and finally permit their spell to probe our hearts, we have not entered into a true contract with the One Who speaks to us. We have not, as spirits, stayed faithful to the Covenant of God. For through His Word throughout the centuries He has reached and revived the soul of man. And if we once have been intoxicated by His utterance, we shall not fail to recognize Him when He speaks again:

> Would ye but sanctify your souls, ye would at this present hour recall that place and those surroundings, and the truth of My utterance should be made evident unto all of you.[2]

The changeless religion of God has not only identified the bonds and interrelationships that shimmer across the space between our diversities but has provided us with a particular capacity to recognize the subtle threads of significance and connection across time also. If we could truly read the import of historical events in the light of the gradual unfoldment of man's spiritual destiny on this planet, we should recognize patterns that must surely develop through the worlds to come. At the same moment, however, we should be summoned by that breadth of perspective to become fully aware of the precious nature of the present hour in our lives. The murmur of the growing seed of our little days, cupped in the hands of this immediate moment, would be rich with the resonance of eternity. Within the groping gestures of our assemblies and communities across the Bahá'í world we should recognize the embryonic promise of the power and beauty of the institutions of the Administrative Order. Within the

partial perceptions we achieve in our relationships between parents and children, within our teaching work, in
the shadow play of our commitments to those with whom
we work, among all the fragments of rivalry and competition, doubt and aggression by which we are con-
fronted, we could begin to decipher the subtle threads and
linked tokens that relate these very fragments to the
Covenant itself. And like the heroes of the Bábí Dispensation we should gradually learn to distinguish, in the
squalid market-place of daily choice, the Station of Him
Who walks before us even as we hear His voice.

This, then, is our goal in acquiring spiritual literacy: to
set our hearts towards the City of Certitude and recognize
arrival by the steps along the way. But even as we breath-
lessly arrive at what appears to be a final stage of con-
clusive argument, we shall surely dive headlong into new
chapters and whole libraries unresearched, and realize
that worlds of God lie far beyond our reach. Increased
knowledge about the lesser covenants between mankind
and the Manifestations of God will tell us more about our
ignorance of the vast and endless Covenant between the
Creator and the souls who circle His throne. The sweetness
of reunion we taste as individuals, when we recognize and
accept the truth of the Bahá'í Faith, is only the first stage
of many separations we shall encounter as we fumble
through the frailties in ourselves and our communities in
our attempts to devote our lives to the development of the
Cause.

Even as we stand in the court of His creative Word, and
hear the accents of His voice, we know that 'At all times I
am near unto thee, but thou art ever far from Me.'[3]
However many words of praise and wonder start to our
lips, we shall sense their feebleness to attempt the azure

flight towards the Infinite, for we are far removed, and can only indicate our Goal by allusions of the outer tongue that barely tell the song of the inner one:

Praise, immeasurable praise be to Thee! I swear by Thy glory! My inner and outer tongue, openly and secretly, testify that Thou hast been exalted above the reach and ken of Thy creatures, above the utterance of Thy servants, above the testimonies of Thy dear ones and Thy chosen ones, and the apprehension of Thy Prophets and of Thy Messengers.[4]

Indeed it is an attribute of God that we should recognize Him by that Name 'which none hath befittingly recognized'.[5] This oblique reference to His power, which measures by our absence of means, satisfies a deep craving in the human heart. It is perhaps for this reason that in the story mentioned earlier we accepted the sky-maiden's lack of protest and self-justification concerning the contents of the basket. Some things cannot be said, and we know that speech would tend to minimize their magnitude. So by sleight of syntax Bahá'u'lláh permits us to indicate the Greatest Name with a gesture that simultaneously frees it from any limitations.

Two Books

One of the earliest principles we learned about spiritual literacy was that it requires a tacit understanding. The pure in heart do not stand up as candidates for public recognition; ceremonies of innocence are not well advertised. The Bahá'í Writings repeatedly stress the validity of an unheard language that tells us of the spirit's motions. Words are not only couched upon the lips but lurk within the very stones at our feet, sigh on the spring breeze and

hum within the marrow bone. They are words that sing in
every fibre of our bodies, as Bahá'u'lláh Himself attests:

My tongue, both the tongue of my body and the tongue of my
heart, my limbs and members, every pulsating vein within me,
every hair of my head, all proclaim . . .[6]

There is a universal symphony that resonates through our
arteries and bones and enables them to vibrate with the
rhythms of the soul. '. . . every bone in my body', says
Bahá'u'lláh, 'soundeth like a pipe'.[7] And again He pro-
claims, 'The limbs of my body testify to Thy unity, and the
hair of my head declareth the power of Thy sovereignty
and might.'[8]

   As a token of His grace, as a sign of His infinite loving-
kindness, He has made every atom a depository of His
secrets, a seal upon His mysteries, for 'The signs of God
shine as manifest and resplendent as the sun amidst the
works of His creatures',[9] and these are signs 'which He,
Himself, hath placed within these realities'.[10] Everything
in this contingent world, which is so symbolic of limitation
and inadequacy, so fragmented and random before the
evidences of His Oneness, is simultaneously pregnant with
potentialities, and infused with a divine energy which, if
read aright, could revitalize our hearts and minds:

Although the spirit is hidden from view, still its commandments
shine out like rays of light upon the world of the human body.
In the same way, although the Kingdom of heaven is hidden
from the sight of this unwitting people, still, to him who seeth
with the inner eye, it is plain as day.[11]

If we could become spiritually literate, therefore, it would
be possible to see the hidden resolutions in the contraries
around us, for to spell out the eternal verities in all things

would enable us to see the connections between these syllables and words:

Therein every man of insight can perceive that which would lead to the Straight Path and would enable him to attain the Great Announcement.[12]

The Manifestations of God have not only been the Bearers of the revealed scrolls of the Revelations of God, providing mankind with the Word which in each dispensation generated a new creation. They have also been the Teachers of the inner tongue, refining our inner ears, and thrilling our hearts with the desire to read for ourselves the 'immemorial mysteries' of the universe around us:

There are two Books: one is the Book of creation and the other is the written Book. The written Book consisteth of the heavenly Books which are revealed to the Prophets of God and have issued forth from the lips of His Manifestations. The Book of creation is the preserved Tablet and the outspread Roll of existence. The Book of Creation is in accord with the written Book.

In the written Book thou canst find chapters and verses, words and letters, and inner means and mysteries are hidden therein. Likewise the Book of creation is the command of God and the respository of divine mysteries. In it there are great signs, universal images, perfect words, exalted symbols and secrets of all things, whether of the past or of the future.

When thou readest the written Book thou wilt become aware of the mysteries of God, but when thou gazest at the Book of creation thou wilt observe the signs, symbols, realities and reflections of the hidden mysteries of the bounties of His Holiness the Incomparable One.[13]

Indeed, our metaphors lie scattered all about us, for the world of creation has its own letters and syllables, words and sentences endowed with those 'necessary and indispensable relationships which exist in the realities of things'.[14]

All these signs are reflected and can be seen in the book of existence, and the scrolls that depict the shape and pattern of the universe are indeed a most great book.[15]

The matter and motion of the spiritual world, therefore, is as close to us as meaning is to syllables and sounds. And the difference between our everyday speech and high poetry is similar to the distinction between the articulation of our domestic souls and the reverberations of the Word of God. As we learn the language of the spirit, we are attended on all sides by a beckoning creation; and the closer we come to recognizing the relationships between apparent contraries, the clearer it will be to us that these resolutions exist in the world of creation even as they are taught to us by the Manifestations of God in the books of Revelation. Bahá'u'lláh affirms,

Look at the world . . . It unveileth the book of its own self before thine eyes and revealeth that which the Pen of thy Lord, the Fashioner, the All-Informed, hath inscribed therein.[16]

And 'Abdu'l-Bahá further clarifies this similarity between the two books and assures us of the hidden resolutions that await us in our daily lives, that are as accessible to us as meaning in a sentence, could we but read:

. . . in the world of the Holy Writ there are letters, words and verses, and likewise in the world of creation there are letters, words and verses . . .
. . . creation is in accord with the written word, and this is certain.[17]

There is poetry implicit, then, in all our pedestrian ways. There is music that can be piped out through each mouldering bone. The arteries that flow within out friendships throb with life, and there is no pebble but resounds. So it is that we hear the voice of the Beloved calling us to assume our part in this duet of love, which will remain inaccessible to us so long as we withhold ourselves from participation in it:

O Son of Being! Love Me, that I may love thee. If thou lovest Me not, My love can in no wise reach thee. Know this, O servant.[18]

The inferential nature of spiritual language, therefore, not only maintains the distance between us and the One Who is far greater 'than the Great One men are wont to call Thee,'[19] but also enables us to enter more fully into the dialogue. We must become active participants who lean forward in response, who commit themselvs to the desire to hear and understand this vital spiritual communication. In other words, by entering the equation we are reminded that we must necessarily remain seekers in relation to God. Only a true seeker's credentials 'of earnest striving, of longing desire, of passionate devotion, of fervid love, of rapture, and ecstasy'[20] can qualify him to read and comprehend the mysteries that are concealed in the creative Word. The silent and allusive nature of this language enables him to participate more closely, though this seems at first to be a mysterious paradox:

Let not your hearts be perturbed, O people, when the glory of My Presence is withdrawn, and the ocean of My utterance is stilled. In My presence amongst you there is a wisdom, and in My absence there is yet another, inscrutable to all but God, the Incomparable, the All-Knowing.[21]

Indeed, the positive value of allusive communication lies

in the fact that it involves the speaker and the listener to an equal degree: as much depends on the sensitivity and responsiveness of the latter as on the precision and selectivity of the former. And since a true resolution of contraries is only possible in a balanced equation, it is not surprising to find in the teachings of the Bahá'í Faith such an emphasis placed on the hearer and the quality of his response to the Word of God. It is moreover an equality in terms of participation in the Covenant, and not with reference to station; once again the emphasis lies in the nature of the response and not in the isolated definitions of the polarities involved. This too is confirmed by the teachings in the Bahá'í Faith regarding our complete equality in the eyes of God, which, however, is distinct from the infinite variety of our diverse capacities, our rank, and potential.

Contraries

In the Hidden Word of Bahá'u'lláh quoted below we find a fascinating interplay between three sets of contraries or pairs which illustrates for us the subtle degrees of difference in the quality of response with which we can approach each other and the Revelation itself. The three metaphors which Bahá'u'lláh employs in a single breath do not at first seem to have much in common, but they all affirm the principle of response without which there would be a complete breakdown in the communication of wisdom, nourishment and love:

O Son of Dust! The wise are they that speak not unless they obtain a hearing, even as the cup-bearer, who proffereth not his cup till he findeth a seeker, and the lover who crieth not out from the depths of his heart until he gazeth upon the beauty of his beloved . . .[22]

The first example introduces the relationship between the Word of God and the heart of man in its most immediate sense as the speaker and the listener. The second identifies the condition of servitude and is implicit throughout the Writings in the imagery of kingship and submission or powerlessness. The third example invites us into the wonderment, the tension, the pain and tenderness implicit in the relationship between lovers, and whose imagery is reflected in the words 'generating influence' and 'impact' throughout the Writings.

By placing these three images side by side, Bahá'u'lláh simultaneously differentiates between them and permits us to allow one to influence our appreciation of the other. The hearer has a passive role to play in relation to the wise one and his listening capacity does not reflect so strongly the yearning and more active desire of the seeker in relation to the cup-bearer. But receptivity and desire find their consummation in the attitude of passionate participation between the lover and the beloved. In spite of these differences in degree, all conditions tell us something of response. And the common factor in all three is that the response could not be one-sided if wisdom is to be conveyed, if wine is to be drunk and love experienced.

Perhaps, too, Bahá'u'lláh's wonderful generosity in offering us three examples for this equation of response, instead of only one, allows us to recognize more easily how fluid are these roles, how flexible should be these relationships. We may find ourselves the 'wise' in some circumstances and be required to learn and listen in others. A seeker too can himself become a cup-bearer towards another, and while we can be active participants in one form of response, we may need to be silent and receptive 'ears' in another. The Manifestation of God is the recipient in His relationship to God and the active, generating influence in His relation to mankind. Indeed, because of this juxtaposition, we begin to recognize that the principle being enunciated here is simply *response*, in all its multiplicity of forms, and so although the equation between tongue and ear is entirely different in type and tone from that between male and female counterparts, yet we are now prepared to meet in the Writings the countless references to the particularly 'feminine' nature of the soul's response to the creative Word.

The imagery of male and female relationships in creation, like those of the tongue and the ear, the light beam and the eye, the sun's rays and the earth, and others, are all aspects of the 'glorious structure' which Bahá'u'lláh identifies in His *Lawḥ-i-Ḥikmat* (Tablet of Wisdom). These also might be said to constitute the pairs referred to by 'Abdu'l-Bahá when He writes: 'From the pairing of even the smallest particles in the world of being are the grace and bounty of God made manifest'.[23] And it is the divorce between such pairs that makes us aware of contraries. This Tablet, which is so rich with mysteries that are both hidden and manifest, seems to be telling us of both the book of Revelation and the book of creation, for it not only holds a mirror to the world around us and describes with utter simplicity the principles at work in this glorious structure, but it also seems, with further study, to identify the powers at work within the Cause itself, which must, if it is to be effective in the world, be attuned to the same basic harmonies.

That which hath been in existence had existed before, but not in the form thou seest today. The world of existence came into being through the heat generated from the interaction between the active force and that which is its recipient. These two are the same, yet they are different. Thus doth the Great Announce-

ment inform thee about this glorious structure. Such as communicate the generating influence and such as receive its
impact are indeed created through the irresistible Word of God
which is the Cause of the entire creation, while all else besides
His Word are but the creatures and the effects thereof. Verily
thy Lord is the Expounder, the All-Wise.[24]

There may be philosophers among Bahá'ís; there may also
be mystics and deep thinkers. But for the most part we are
simple folk and respond to basic concepts. The power of
the Cause of God is such that it can transmute our simplicity and the basic concepts that we are familiar with
into the most profound philosophies. We are being summoned to response from every level of comprehension and
Bahá'u'lláh's language most lucidly invites us into the
high halls of abstraction, all the while encouraging us to
marvel at the rich mosaic at our feet, the lustre of the
pillars at each side, the wonder of the solid walls of our
own dependable experience round about.

We are all familiar with the difference between giver
and receiver, for in our families, in our marriages, in our
communities, and in our work we find ourselves assuming
one or other role. We know our roles cannot be rigid, for
it is the interplay between the 'active force' and its
'recipient' that creates the excitement we experience when
we tell someone of the Faith and then hear him sharing the
message with another, so that we ourselves become the
learner at a new level of discovery. We also know that it is
the quality of response between the giver and the receiver
that constitutes the real gift, for if there is no deep commitment in the giving, and no heartfelt desire in the
receiving, the object that is passed between us remains
dead, inert and cold. Indeed, when there is no sincere
response, either as a hearer or as a seeker or as a lover, the
gift that is offered itself becomes a cause of separation

between two people even as the structure of religion should be abandoned, according to Bahá'u'lláh, when it disrupts the ancient principle of response between human beings and the soul and its God.

All these principles of response between giver and receiver, between speaker and spoken-to, between the soul and its Beloved, are couched in the clarity of Bahá'u'lláh's language, which identifies these pairs as 'such as communicate the generating influence and such as receive its impact'.[25] In this Tablet we discover, therefore, that contraries are not being watered down and diluted into a dull compromise. They are being invited instead to participate fully in a fusion or marriage which will itself generate a heat that will inspire our minds to a wider understanding, merge our hearts into a sphere of unity, and give birth to a world order that has been the dream of mystics and philosophers of all past ages.

The following chapters, therefore, will explore the theme of response on three levels simultaneously: that of communication between tongue and ear, the complementary roles reflected in the Writings between men and women, and the rights of the individual within the Bahá'í Administrative Order. Throughout the book emphasis will rest, not on the rigidity of these polarities, but on the complementary dance between them; not on a static representation of types in society or within the individual psyche, but the flow and interchange, the collaboration and creativity, that they inspire. All differences and contrasts, moreover, being metaphor, also remind us that we are in the Kingdom of Names, where the approximation of 'even so' is as close as we can get to the comprehension of forces beyond us, for 'minds cannot grasp Me nor hearts contain Me.'[26]

CHAPTER TWO

The Hearing Ear

THE WRITINGS of the Bahá'í Revelation abound with references to words. The wealth of written treasures that we have from the pen of Bahá'u'lláh is witness enough to the potency He has placed within this medium of communication. The symbol of the Word as the Intercessor between the Ancient of Days and the soul of man has reached the zenith of its powers in the abundance of words whose mysteries lie waiting for us to unravel in this day:

No man of wisdom can demonstrate his knowledge save by means of words. This showeth the significance of the Word as is affirmed in all the Scriptures, whether of former times or more recently. For it is through its potency and animating spirit that the people of the world have attained so eminent a position.[1]

And so we may assume, as the smaller reflects the greater in this universe of interrelationships, that amongst ourselves too there have been released powers of communication, elucidation and clear connection that have not been so accessible to man before, owing to his relative immaturity. And Bahá'u'lláh is specific in His guidance on this matter, stressing that 'words and utterances should be both impressive and penetrating'.[2]

But all this surely has profound implications in terms of

our capacity to hear and respond, for speech is only part of
the equation. Bahá'u'lláh reminds us of this when He says
that 'no word will be infused with these two qualities
unless it be uttered wholly for the sake of God and with
due regard unto the exigencies of the occasion and the
people.'[2] As an audience we are used to being wooed and
seduced in order to respond positively to what we hear,
but how are we prepared on this occasion to greet the
summons of joy, the secrets of intimacy from the pen of
Bahá'u'lláh? How ready are we to turn towards each other
with a sensitivity that is worthy of our station? In our cities
we see the loneliness caused by indifferent or negative
response in all kinds of forms. In our immediate communities, lack of the right response between individuals
causes some of us to shield our shyness in shells of silence,
and others to look for approximations of spontaneity in
attitudes of chattering geniality. Within the intimacy of
our families we have all experienced the difference between the glowing confirmation of loving response, and
the desert of alienation when it is eclipsed. We have suffered on the one hand from the insensitivity of those who
seemed not to hear, and on the other been burdened by
the heavy demand made for response. This concept is so
vital that the Word of God itself remains sealed in silent
dependence upon the quality and sincerity of our response
for its utterance to be effective.

Bahá'u'lláh attests that 'Man's treasure is his utterance', but continues immediately, 'yet this Wronged One
hath withheld His Tongue, for the disbelievers are lying in
ambush . . .'[3] It is not the Word that is diminished by our
folly, but we who are bitterly deprived. Our inability to
hear 'the king of words' withholds us from an ocean of
riches, but it does not limit the pervasive influence of this

ocean which comprehends all things in the 'realm of being'.[4]

The Great Being saith: The Word is the master key for the whole world, inasmuch as through its potency the doors of the hearts of men, which in reality are the doors of heaven, are unlocked.[5]

Lamentations and Betrayal

To be inadequate listeners, unresponsive readers, and perverse enough to lie in ambush rather than lean in anticipation towards the utterance of the Pen of Glory, condemns us to a terrible separation. We lie bound in prisons of our own making, the master key tossed from our hands; we find ourselves exiles in inward lands of lost communication, for to break the ancient bond between the reflective soul and its Source of light has fearful consequences. When in the *Hidden Words*[6] we read that the immortal Being returned with lamentation and weeping from the hill of faithfulness, we realize that the answer to the question, 'Why the wailing and weeping?' is simply that there had been no response. Humanity as a whole has betrayed its trust, and the few who responded were sacrificed for doing so. The world had not heard, had not received. And in this breach, love, wine, and wisdom remain unconveyed.

In a passage that addresses this question in *The Promised Day is Come*, Shoghi Effendi selects examples of the verbal response to the message of Bahá'u'lláh in phrases that appal by their forceful rejection. 'What manner of welcome did [the world] accord Him,' he asks, 'and what response did His call evoke?' And then we hear the reply:

'Unmitigated indifference . . . unrelenting hatred . . . scornful derision . . . utter contempt . . . condemnations pronounced, threats hurled, and . . . banishments decreed . . .'[7] Bahá'u'lláh Himself gives us a similar review of the response meted out to the Báb:

> No sooner did He reveal Himself, than all the people rose up against Him. By some He was denounced as one that hath uttered slanders against God, the Almighty, the Ancient of Days. Others regarded Him as a man smitten with madness, an allegation which I, Myself, have heard from the lips of one of the divines. Still others disputed His claim . . . , and stigmatized Him as one who had stolen and used as his the words of the Almighty, who had perverted their meaning, and mingled them with his own. The Eye of Grandeur weepeth sore for the things which their mouths have uttered, . . .[8]

The lamentations in Bahá'u'lláh's *Prayers and Meditations* are almost all provoked by humanity's lack of response to His Revelation. His sorrowful sense of exile is as a result of this rejection; His loneliness and grief are caused by the insensitivity of His hearers. The prisons in which He lies have been digged by their superstitions and idle fancies; at morning and evening He is attended by the 'darts of their envy, and . . . the spears of their hate'. Long after we can no longer sustain the anguish He experiences from 'the wrongs committed by such of Thy creatures as have turned their backs to Thee', there is still tribulation upon tribulation heaped upon Him by the ignorance of those who do not hear, and by the sullen lack of response of those who do not understand. Even our own inability to comprehend the degree to which He is 'grievously touched' oppresss us with a sense of our having failed to attend His call from the hill of faithfulness.[9]

One of the most confounding examples of our lack of

response, in the *Hidden Words*, is contained in those images of anguish and intimacy where we see the Divine Spirit hovering above the couch of a heedless humanity. That this profoundly spiritual state of being should be conveyed to us through the metaphors of sexual alienation tells us something vital about the nature of response between apparent contraries in the world. For the callousness evinced by man, who remains 'busied with others than Myself', is so great that the Spirit bewails his plight and abandons him to return 'whence it came'.[10] The reference, of course, could also be to man's own betrayed soul, but at whatever level we might understand this mysterious removal, the sense we all share is how great a desolation it can cause. It is so great a breach, in fact, that it may not be uttered for shame. Indeed, this sense of shame will attend us through all the worlds of God, as it would, too, if man and woman were to betray the single soul of companionship within their marriage and instead 'live out their lives in great bitterness, longing at every moment for death', for they would 'be shamefaced in the heavenly realm'.[11]

If this is the consequence of the lesser betrayal, what can be said of the greater?

O Essence of Desire! At many a dawn have I turned from the realms of the Placeless unto thine abode, and found thee on the bed of ease busied with others than Myself. Thereupon, even as the flash of the spirit, I returned to the realms of celestial glory and breathed it not in My retreats above unto the hosts of holiness.[12]

When Bahá'u'lláh turned His back on the Bábí community in Baghdád and sought refuge for His sorrowing soul in the deserted wildernesses of Sulaymáníyyih, it was because He had 'tarried amongst this people, and failed to discern the slightest response on their part'.[13] His broken-hearted anguish is such that the sight of Him seems to transfix the sun and stop its rising, causing an eyewitness to tremble with dread:

... he had on one occasion seen Him, between dawn and sunrise, suddenly come out from His house, His night-cap still on His head, showing such signs of perturbation that he was powerless to gaze into His face. . . . 'I stood,' declared Mírzá Áqá Ján, 'rooted to the spot, lifeless, dried up as a dead tree, ready to fall under the impact of the stunning power of His words.'[14]

When the life-giving spirit is withdrawn as a result of our own failure to respond to it, our very souls wither to the hollow root. Standing with Mírzá Áqá Ján at the grey hour of the heart's daybreak, we hear the dry whisper of our withering hopes, we see our life's horizon stark before us, and all about, the trees that stand blasted, leafless and unresponsive to the rising sun. It is a landscape that troubles us with its familiarity; it is an inner place where our unreceptive spirits have sometimes roamed. And faced by the 'utmost sadness' of the Manifestation of God, we recognize it immediately. The nameless betrayals of our inner lives, like the people's lack of response in Baghdád on that occasion, cause Bahá'u'lláh, 'even as the flash of the spirit', to retreat from our heedlessness with a pain and sense of rejection of which we can barely conceive in our limited physical terms. In His own words, 'Our withdrawal . . . contemplated no return, and Our separation hoped for no reunion.'[15]

The Need for Response

Yet the mercy of God exceeds His wrath, and His patience outlasts His weariness of us; although the earth itself shuns our arrogance, the winds of Divine grace continue to blow. After a sojourn of two years in the mountains of Sulaymáníyyih, Bahá'u'lláh received a summons 'From the Mystic Source . . . bidding Us return whence We came. Surrendering Our will to His, We submitted to His injunction.'[16] And in the same way, although we fail repeatedly in the quality of our response to the Revelation, its beauty still attends us, its compassion still accompanies our deeds, and its call still summons us to praise and service:

Every time I hold my peace, and cease to extol Thy wondrous virtues, Thy Spirit impelleth me to cry out before all who are in Thy heaven and on Thy earth; and every time I am still, the breaths wafted from the right hand of Thy will and purpose pass over me, and stir me up, and I find myself to be as a leaf which lieth at the mercy of the winds of Thy decree, and is carried away whithersoever Thou dost permit or command it.[17]

Bahá'u'lláh teaches us the ideal relationship between speaker and spoken-to by His own commitment to the winds of Divine Will. No degree of separation or rejection can still their surging in His heart, and so His lamentations about the lack of a hearing ear are tempered by His exultant songs of praise in response, on His own part, to the unconcealed splendour of the magnitude of God in creation:

I am well aware, O my Lord, that I have been so carried away by the clear tokens of Thy loving-kindness, and so completely inebriated with the wine of Thine utterance, that whatever I behold I readily discover that it maketh Thee known unto me, and it remindeth me of Thy signs, and of Thy tokens, and of Thy testimonies.[18]

The extremity of anguish which the Manifestation of God

endures when there is 'no ear to hear, nor heart to understand' finds its most poignant human expression in the
voice of 'Abdu'l-Bahá, who also endures His vigil on the
hill of faithfulness, waiting for humanity's response to the
call of God in this Day:

O ye the cherished loved ones of 'Abdu'l-Bahá! It is a long time
now since my inward ear hath heard any sweet melodies out of
certain regions, or my heart been gladdened; and this despite
the fact that ye are ever present in my thoughts and standing
clearly visible before my sight. Filled to overflowing is the goblet
of my heart with the wine of the love I bear you, and my
yearning to set eyes upon you streameth like the spirit through
my arteries and veins. From this it is clear how great is my
affliction.[19]

In this heartfelt expression of longing for response we can
see the traces of all three conditions referred to in the
previous chapter: those of the lover, the cup-bearer, and
the wise one whose words remain unheeded. In the person
of 'Abdu'l-Bahá we also meet the mingling of the 'generating force' and its 'recipient', for while it is His tongue
that utters the expression of longing, it is His inward ear
which leans to hear our response; while He is the cup-
bearer who stands brimming with confirmations for us, He
is also the receptacle that bears the grace, contains the
favour, and waits to be lifted to our lips; and finally,
though He is flooded with love He is parched also for 'the
cherished . . . ones' to turn to Him:

Sleepless I toss and turn upon my bed, mine eyes straining to
behold the morning light of faithfulness and trust. I agonize
even as a fish, its inward parts afire as it leapeth about in terror
upon the sand, yet I ever look for Thy bestowals to appear from
every side.[20]

It is because of 'Abdu'l-Bahá's exquisite ability to echo the human condition that we are helped to learn from Him what our role must be in relation to Bahá'u'lláh. The relationship between Them is frequently referred to in the Writings as that of the sun and moon. All the connotations related to the Perfect Exemplar, the reflection of the light of Bahá, and the Mystery of God – descriptions of 'Abdu'l-Bahá – are couched in this metaphor. The traditional 'feminine' attributes of the moon in relation to the generative influence of the sun are also implicit in some measure, and find their culmination in Shoghi Effendi's description, in *God Passes By*, of the parental roles of these twin Figures in the genesis of the Administrative Order. Bearing these relationships in mind, it is significant to note that in one of His prayers revealed for marriage 'Abdu'l-Bahá refers to both man and woman as orbs reflecting the light of God, 'wedded in Thy love, conjoined in servitude to Thy Holy Threshold, united in ministering to Thy Cause'.[21] They are, therefore, initially in the receptive role since their marriage is sanctified first and foremost in relation to the Will of God, rather than to each other.

It would seem, with 'Abdu'l-Bahá as our Example, that the traditional concepts of passivity, inferiority and negativity associated with the moon are completely redefined in this Revelation. It is neither a remote, allusive and mysterious element at work upon our lives, nor a source of evil and ill-will, contrary qualities applied both to the moon and to women in the past. We have, in this space-spanning generation, become more familiar with the moon and the capacities of women too, and are prepared perhaps to discover new definitions and to learn subtle differences which this Revelation has identified in the conventional symbolism of the sexes.

A Perfect Listener

In order to approach one of the facets of this reflective
quality symbolized by the moon, we might wonder awhile
at the mysterious nature of the Greatest Holy Leaf,
Bahá'íyyih <u>Kh</u>ánum, in whose life it is possible to recognize some of the qualities which make of her Brother the
Mystery of God.

This extraordinary woman, whose characteristics of
frailty and indomitable strength combined to make her a
legend in the history of the Cause, and give her a unique
station in the Bahá'í Dispensation, is addressed by Bahá'u'-
lláh in unequivocally exalted terms:

Verily, We have elevated thee to the rank of one of the most
distinguished among thy sex, and granted thee, in My court, a
station such as none other woman hath surpassed.[22]

This station seems to be one of exquisite reflection. Her
spirit and body bend in response and bear witness to the
Revelation of her glorious Father. She is the perfectly
tuned ear that leans and hearkens to the melodies of the
Manifestation of God. She is the luminous eye on whose
horizons the Sun of His Revelation casts its beams. Her
body, more like a fragment of her soul, is first to cleave and
bow down before His authority. She is the enactment of
ideal recipience; the purpose of her existence is to testify to
the generative powers of God. Bahá'u'lláh indicates that
her 'feminine role' is none other than to be enamoured of
the Primal Will, and even gives her a love-song to this
purpose:

Let these exalted words be thy love-song on the tree of Bahá, O
thou most holy and resplendent Leaf: 'God, besides Whom is

none other God, the Lord of this world and the next![23]

He Himself sings her a paean of praise precisely because of her capacity to reflect and respond, receive and irradiate His blessings:

How sweet thy presence before Me; how sweet to gaze upon thy face, to bestow upon thee My loving-kindness, to favor thee with My tender care, to make mention of thee in this, My Tablet – a Tablet which I have ordained as a token of My hidden and manifest grace unto thee.[24]

The Greatest Holy Leaf was, in one sense, a symbol of one dwelling in paradise, as defined by the Báb. For in the Tablet quoted above, Bahá'u'lláh addresses His daughter in terms that bear a striking resemblance to the conditions which the Báb enumerates: to be exposed to the Manifestation, to hear His verses and believe, to attain His presence and receive His good-pleasure, to taste the fruits of His Oneness.[25] Exposed to God's Manifestation in such close kinship, the Greatest Holy Leaf indeed heard, believed and received the full sweetness of His Message:

We have created thine eyes to behold the light of My countenance, thine ears to hearken unto the melody of My words, thy body to pay homage before My throne.[26]

And finally she 'tasted of the sweet savours of My holy, My wondrous pleasure' and drank the soul's sweetness 'from My honeyed mouth . . .'[27]

Thus she becomes an exquisite example of that particularly 'feminine' relationship of a soul to its Creator, and simultaneously the ideal symbol of the 'guided soul' in response to the Cause of Bahá'u'lláh. No wonder, therefore, that her spirit becomes a vital influence upon us in this society divided by distressing vicissitudes, or that her memory, according to Shoghi Effendi, is 'an inspiration and a solace amid the wreckage of a sadly shaken world'.[28] For unless humanity can turn whole-heartedly and reflect the truth of this Cause by emulating her example, its fortunes are in hazard. And until, like her, we are able to re-evaluate our concepts of power and authority, and re-create individually as well as in society the harmonious interaction between our complementary roles, we shall only understand to a limited degree that pre-existent order to which Bahá'u'lláh is recalling us when He says, 'Thus doth the Great Announcement inform thee about this glorious structure.'[29]

The Mystery of Reversal

It is not in keeping with the contemporary tone of liberal-mindedness that we should be recalled. It seems much more fashionable to introduce the Faith to our friends as a force that impels us to look into the future than one which requires reconsideration of the past. Our short-sightedness tends to limit vision whether we are looking into the future or into the past, however, and so we often confuse the pre-existent order, identified with a universal time-scale, with a human order identified with a local time-scale of six thousand years of 'civilized' history on this planet. Bahá'u'-lláh's 'glorious structure' has more in common with the birth and death of stars than the rise and fall of fashions in liberal-mindedness. And so we need to remind ourselves that, whichever way our past or present aberrations may be influencing us, the Manifestation of God is recalling vast principles of order to us that are in silent motion in the universe around, which through a thousand imperceptible ways must influence the texture of our threaded lives.

We cannot confuse the quality of the life of the Greatest Holy Leaf, therefore, with notions of current psychology that look back only a few thousand years, and interpret the future of society in terms of human civilization rather than spiritual evolution. She is being identified for us as a symbol of a far more pervasive order at work in the universe: she is a reminder of a spiritual pattern by which human civilization must develop. A fuller appreciation of her significance requires that conventional prejudices and contemporary reactions both be reversed. This may be one of the meanings implicit in the 'mystery of the Great Reversal', which is a term used by Shaykh Aḥmad and clarified by Bahá'u'lláh Himself in the *Kitáb-i-Aqdas*.* According to 'Abdu'l-Bahá, the winds of this Revelation have reversed the mighty banners of authority and established the 'most exalted standard' of entirely different priorities.[31] The Law of God itself, which has so often been a symbol of dictatorial authority in paternalistic societies in the past, is identified by 'Abdu'l-Bahá as a woman,[32] and so it does not surprise us to find that during the last years of her life, the Greatest Holy Leaf was the only person trusted by Shoghi Effendi to hold the reins of authority and govern the affairs of the Bahá'í world while he prepared himself for his great undertaking of Guardianship. The meaning of 'reversal', therefore, is not a superficial exchange of roles, but a command that we become fluid in our capacities and rise and meet what the occasion demands of us. For by this flexibility the concept of response is sanctified: it is not who we are but what we do in

---

* In one of His Tablets Bahá'u'lláh explains that the Mystery of the Reversal is a reference to the principle that those in exalted positions shall be abased, and they who are abased shall be exalted.[30]

relation to each other that makes a jewel of our lives.

No individual, therefore, can symbolize the active force alone, or assume the role of the receptive agent rigidly. Just as it is vital for each one of us to nurture and possess this praiseworthy quality of receptivity, so too the Writings stress the need for us to initiate our own response to them in action. The mystery of reversal, which is so startling in its implications with regard to the relationship between men and women, as well as in the equation of power and communication, is that it requires an inter-cessor to take effect. There has to be an intermediary, an advocate or a catalyst to enable the fluid shift of roles to take place. In the spiritual equation between God and the soul of man this Intercessor is the Divine Luminary Him-self, who is Bahá'u'lláh in this day. In the gulf of human relationships, 'Abdu'l-Bahá steps in and conveys us to each other in a manner that enables us to see Him between us in that meeting. In the vacuum between tongue and ear, language is the go-between; and between men and women love allows reversals that enable them to grow.

It confirms this principle to discover that in his love-poem,[33] written at her passing in July 1932, Shoghi Effendi addresses the Greatest Holy Leaf, that pure sym-bol of the listening ear, the undivided response, as the generative power herself. She becomes the bearer of the message, the intercessor between the 'toiling masses of thy ardent lovers', (among whom Shoghi Effendi includes him-self), and her glorious Father, Bahá'u'lláh. She takes on, in the last phase of her life, which the Guardian beautifully reflects in the last paragraphs of his eulogy to her, the role, the force, the attributes of the medium between man and God. And mysteriously, the motion has also been reversed. She who symbolized the soul in its response to her Creator becomes the means by which 'we whose souls have been impregnated by the energizing influence of her love' can pledge ourselves before the mercy-seat of Bahá'u'lláh. 'Bear thou this my message to 'Abdu'l-Bahá,' he tells her, and then in a touching gesture of total dependence and reliance, he offers her the words by which she can address the Centre of the Covenant. Thus she becomes the eloquent champion of the drama of the Cause; she steps forward to play the part of advocate. But the significance in this reversal is that it has been Shoghi Effendi himself who enabled her to assume this powerful role.

The complementary nature of the generating influence and that which receives its impact is profoundly subtle and reaches deep. To comprehend more fully the manner in which each releases the capacities of the other, it may be useful to look more closely at the principle of advocacy which is contained in the Writings, and which must surely find its reflection in the nature of our institutions and our lives.

CHAPTER THREE

Advocacy

To SPEAK on behalf of others is less valued in our strident
society than to speak for ourselves. Indeed, many who
would consider themselves subjugated have too recently
found an authentic voice to be able so soon to abandon it.
For we have so often been forced into silence by our
helplessness and anger that we can no longer choose
silence freely as an alternative to verbal and literal force.
The dilemma for many people is whether or not they
should redress the wrongs in society by force and coercion,
when force and coercion have been the cause of most
wrongs and have been known to bear only these same
fruits. 'Abdu'l-Bahá tells us quietly and unequivocally
that, 'In this, the cycle of Almighty God, violence and
force, constraint and oppression, are one and all con-
demned,'[1] which, while relieving our hearts initially, still
leaves us uncertain how to act. And so we often find
ourselves feeling powerless and ineffective in society,
unable to avert injustice on an individual level, and para-
lyzed by our own guilt and by other people's accusations
that our lack of strident protest is impotent passivity.

Shoghi Effendi articulates this very condition, and enables us to assess it in perspective without undermining how we feel, when he writes:

Dangers, however sinister, . . . Strife and confusion, however bewildering . . . Tribulations, however afflictive, . . . Denunciations, however clamorous, . . . Upheavals, however cataclysmic, must never deflect their course.[2]

The teachings of Bahá'u'lláh, therefore, give us the confidence born of a broader perspective, without which so much of what we say or do would remain futile. They remind us that, while our afflictions or humiliations beg for voice, if they are expressed in ignorance or defiance of the response they will receive, the effect will also be futile. Bahá'u'lláh admonishes us:

Every word is endowed with a spirit, therefore the speaker or expounder should carefully deliver his words at the appropriate time and place, for the impression which each word maketh is clearly evident and perceptible. The Great Being saith: One word may be likened unto fire, another unto light, and the influence which both exert is manifest in the world.[3]

If this is true of words, it is surely applicable to actions, and even as the fires of outrage burn about us, the contrast between their flames and the pure light of the Word of God cannot but be evident.

While the convulsions of the heaving world render us helpless at times, we might remember how much greater was the isolation of the Mouthpiece of the Word of God amidst this chaos. For if we, in our own circumstances, have felt helpless and angry, have been forced into silence on the one hand and driven ourselves into strident protest on the other, and all the time felt our powerlessness to be effective in society, then how much more must the Manifestation of God Himself have endured, in the face of a heedless and arrogant humanity who neither recognized His presence nor responded to His message, and who not only stopped their ears to His call but flung Him to the furthest corners of civilization in order to avoid the urgency of His appeal.

What language should He Who is the Mouthpiece of God choose to speak, so that they who are shut out as by a veil from Him can recognize His glory?[4]

His anguish is nowhere so articulate as in His prayers and meditations, which of all His Writings seem most to cry out for a fit hearer:

Unseal the lips of Thy will, O my Lord, and let a word proceed therefrom that shall subject unto itself the world and all that is therein. How long shalt Thou behold these things and tarry, O my God?[5]

It is precisely because His sufferings loom as large as His powerlessness that we are able to identify so closely with Him, to feel such awesome familiarity with His distress, to find our cries silenced before the resonating thrill of His appeal:

How long shalt Thou remain seated, O my God, on the throne of Thy forbearance and patience? Speak Thou Thy word of wrath, O Thou Whom no eyes can see![6]

Not only does He give voice to our deepest human needs to have injustice acknowledged and oppression known, but He becomes our advocate. He speaks on our behalf. He places all His own affliction to one side, and steps forward to bear witness to the anguish of our hearts:

I swear by Thy glory! My lamentations are not for the things which have befallen me in Thy path, but are due to my recognition that by reason of mine abasement the hearts of them that love Thee have been sore shaken . . .[7]

And in the exquisite prayer He has revealed in recognition of the souls 'like the angels which Thou hast created of snow and of fire',[8] He once again becomes the Spokesman of their sufferings, the Intercessor for the wrongs they have sustained:

All hope is ready to be extinguished in the hearts of Thy chosen ones, O my God! Where are the breezes of Thy grace? They are hemmed in on all sides by their enemies; where are the ensigns of Thy triumph which Thou didst promise in Thy tablets?[9]

Finally, with a compassion and gentleness that leave us speechless, with our protestations mute, He concludes, '. . . Thou knowest full well the frailty of some of them, and art aware of their impatience in their sufferings.'[10]

It is in this gesture of advocacy which the Manifestation of God assumes on our behalf that we might discover an attitude that does not contain the implications of attack, thereby falling itself a victim to the decrepit formula of power by domination. We need to have heard the sighing of the poor in order to tell the rich about it, but, here again, the poor are not making strident claims about their poverty. For the aim in the telling is to raise the sleeping will from its couch of heedlessness, to shake the torpid conscience and alert the isolated heart to the vibrations of His waiting Will. This end cannot be achieved by force or coercion, and so in the same connection, 'sharing is a personally chosen righteous act: that is, the rich should extend assistance to the poor, . . . but of their own free will, and not because the poor have gained this end by force.'[11]

To speak on another's behalf, therefore, becomes a means of releasing power in a way that self-defence and personal assertiveness could never do. The Short Obligatory Prayer teaches us the simplest form of this equation, for in it we daily become the chief witness of the human condition and stand to testify to what we have understood of our purpose on the planet. Thus the gesture of advocacy He has taught is at once a condition of complete responsibility for oneself, and at the same time of concern for the requirements around us.

The recognition and vindication of the sufferings of others is an activity which the Writings would seem to imply is vital for the enhancement of society's consciousness and the development of humanity's sense of justice. Perhaps it is for this reason that Bahá'u'lláh and 'Abdu'l-Bahá both give poignant expression to the suffering, the patient endurance, the sheer loneliness of the lives, so sweetened by servitude, evinced by such women as Navváb and the Greatest Holy Leaf. In a letter of tender intimacy to His sister, 'Abdu'l-Bahá writes:

Day and night thou livest in my memory. Whenever I remember thee my heart swelleth with sadness and my regret groweth more intense . . . Not for one moment do I cease to remember thee. My sorrow and regret concern not myself; they center around thee. Whenever I recall thine afflictions, tears that I cannot repress rain down from mine eyes . . .[12]

Perhaps the empathy of His responsive heart and the homage of His tongue account for the unreserved tranquillity of His sister's acquiescence, and her triumphant role as the recipient of her Father's message. There is a wisdom and a mystery in her silence that is inscrutable and might leave us perturbed, were we not conscious, as a result of 'Abdu'l-Bahá's homage to her, that because of this, we feel no protest rising to our lips. Had she protested about her afflictions, frustrations, deprivations, there would have been no need for such a tender and eloquent advocate as 'Abdu'l-Bahá. As it is, her very silence, which is far from being passive, enables Him to rise to her defence. Her unspeaking spirit, therefore, becomes the cause and provides the purpose for communication, while separation from her seems so to intensify His sorrow that even communication is annulled:

I dare make no mention of the feelings which separation from her has aroused in mine heart; for whatever I should attempt to express in writing will assuredly be effaced by the tears which such sentiments must bring to mine eyes.[13]

The mystery of their reciprocal relationship is such that the expression of His anguish on her behalf relieves our hearts, and strengthens our own capacity to fulfil her role in our limited lives. For with such an advocate who could refuse to rush towards silence? With such a sensitivity witnessing our servitude who would choose to demand power over another? We could of course stand forward in our own defence and use all means of mind to justify our actions, but in doing so too earnestly, might we relinquish His vindication, His defence? 'Manifold are her sorrows, and infinitely grievous her distress',[14] He says in a prayer He reveals on her behalf; and in a letter to His own daughter, Ḍíyá, He writes: '. . . for all her days she was denied a moment of tranquillity. She was astir and restless every hour of her life.'[15]

The Inner Voice

There is an extraordinary force released when receptivity is so refined that the voice of our inmost soul finds itself expressed from another's lips. Perhaps because the principle of affiliation and close integration is thus reaffirmed, we find the result of such advocacy is more than the sum of the facts that are being conveyed.

We have, in 'Abdu'l-Bahá's talks, a wealth of wisdom and encouragement, appeal and exhortation that cannot be drained of perpetually fresh significance. But there is a subtle spell that takes hold of our listening when we are drawn into the powerful theatre constructed by Shoghi Effendi's pen and find ourselves hearing, not 'Abdu'l-Bahá Himself, but the words His grandson utters on His behalf: 'We can dimly picture to ourselves', the Guardian writes, placing us among the audience, the crowd who gathered around the Master listening to His last farewell, 'the wishes that must have welled from His eager heart . . .'[16] Shoghi Effendi is a mosaic master in the art of setting each jewelled quotation within the context of his own prose. Had he wanted to do so, he could have quoted directly from the talks of 'Abdu'l-Bahá which conveyed just such wishes concerning the future of that promising country of America. But instead, the Guardian deliberately invites us to hear the unspoken yearnings of the Master's heart. By asking us to participate imaginatively in this touching farewell scene, he ensures that we have whole-heartedly responded to the magnitude of our commitments to the Master. By speaking on His behalf he enables us to hear the Master's voice from within ourselves. The quotation marks that distance us from Him are removed, and the audience themselves have become the actors:

An inscrutable Wisdom, we can well imagine Him remark to His disciples on the eve of His departure, has, in His infinite bounty singled out your native land for the execution of a mighty purpose.[17]

What Wisdom can it be that makes us lean so wonderingly across the tar-stained quay of time and space? How mysteriously that Voice calls to us, distanced by the waves that rise from the widening sea! Through the spray we glimpse the white robe fluttering and the glint of sunlight resting on those upraised hands, lifting always, with motions of winged hope, and summoning our hearts to respond to Him. The taste of salt is on our lips. Can we bear to part with Him so easily? May we not leap into the sea and return with Him to the land of our heart's desire? But we have to turn aside, for the words are lost in the salt breeze, the ship is shrouded in mist and He has gone – and so it is with surprise that we discover we are already back in our own lives, with Shoghi Effendi's words before us and *God Passes By* open where we read.

This subtle reversal enables the native land of our limited hearts to become the place where the Master's footsteps might echo, where His voice might yet be heard. When we respond whole-heartedly to His hopes expressed in these words of Shoghi Effendi, when we ourselves become the advocates on His behalf and remember the disappointments He sustained, a resonance takes hold of us that seems to peal out to the sky. We find ourselves echoing chords that are beyond our solitary capacities. It is a process that 'Abdu'l-Bahá Himself indicates for us when He exhorts us to speak well of each other, for when 'a person setteth about . . . opening his lips to praise another, he will touch an answering chord in his hearers and they will be stirred up by the breathings of God.'[18]

And at the same time as we are stirred by these harmonies, we become aware of the smallness of our hopes compared with His, and the paltry nature of our deprivations. Bahá'u'lláh Himself discloses a pattern of humility and a sense of inadequacy that occur even as the advocate stands up to speak. For even though he may be a vital link, indeed a necessary catalyst for resolution to take place, the advocate must also sense himself to be a substitute, a conveyer of means rather than a supplier of ends. He can never be the person on whose behalf he speaks; he can never entirely attain the station towards which he points:

And at whatever time my pen ascribeth glory to any one of Thy names, methinks I can hear the voice of its lamentation in its remoteness from Thee, and can recognize its cry because of its separation from Thy Self.[19]

Although this has profound and mystical connotations, it is equally true in our pedestrian lives. Once again Bahá'u'-lláh speaks in a way that makes a philosopher and a railway porter comprehend the same principle; indeed, He speaks with such a power that the railway porter can think like a philosopher and the philosopher can, if his intellect allows, see life from the point of view of a railway porter. For, no matter who we are, we have all had the experience of trying to put an idea of great value to us into language that expressed its full meaning to another. Whenever we find ourselves telling someone of the majesty of the Cause, we hear the inner voice crying from the heart to say, 'Oh no! No! No! You haven't said it right!' Whenever we want to express an idea that seems very important during a consultation, which we feel compelled to share with a Spiritual Assembly, our hearts sink even as we hear the words stumble on our lips, for that was not what we meant at all, not at all! The words, which are the vehicles of our meaning, let us down; we who are the witnesses of the glory of the Cause, or the spokesmen in an Assembly, or the advocates for the sufferings and needs of a divided world, feel ourselves to be failures.

The wonder of this is, however, that unless the advocate or intercessor feels his humility in the face of all that is not said, he would be in danger of becoming an untrustworthy channel, would speak on behalf of his own ego only. The doors of his sensitivity must be open wide, both to speak with accuracy and to respond to all he cannot say. Advocacy, therefore, is a transparent responsibility and requires a clear-eyed core of self-knowledge which connects our hearts to the nerve-centre of our relationship with our Creator. Detached from personal vindication and fearless for the sake of a wider Cause, for a larger purpose than anything our own lives might express, the spirit of advocacy within us becomes light and untrammelled as the breeze, a purveyor of relief, a breath of magnanimity to those who encounter it. Characterized by the fear of God, steadfastness to the Covenant, and detachment from the divisive mental habits of the world, this condition has been best symbolized amongst humanity within the station of the Hands of the Cause of God. Appointed by Shoghi Effendi, they spoke on his behalf at gatherings throughout the Bahá'í world, repeated his urgent appeals, stimulated response to his messages, stirred the hearts of the Bahá'ís with the fragrance of devotion, so that his goals might be fulfilled and happiness be brought to his heart. And bearing in mind the transparency of the advocate, we turn to God and offer salutation to the Hands of the Cause,

through whom the light of fortitude hath shone forth and the truth hath been established that the authority to choose rests with God, the Powerful, the Mighty, the Unconstrained.[20]

It overwhelms us to realize the delicacy of feeling with

which Bahá'u'lláh speaks on behalf of the human race, for in spite of the rejection and lack of response He has received from our hands, He is eagerly looking amongst us for examples to praise. Indeed, it is because we know full well the magnitude of His own endurance and suffering compared with ours, and are conscious of the countless silent ones whose lives cupped the jewelled wine of martyrdom and servitude, that we are dumbfounded by His magnanimity as He stoops down Himself to be our advocate. Pausing at the city gate of the Land of Ṭá* He asks, 'Which one of the multitude of thy sincere lovers shall We remember . . . ?' and indicates to posterity the blood of 'the victims of tyranny . . . concealed beneath thy soil',[21] Bahá'u'lláh also chooses to commemorate His own sister, who otherwise would have remained nameless among the rest, 'as a token of Our fidelity, and as a proof of Our loving-kindness, unto her'.[22] This then is the response to those who choose to keep their bond of trust with Him on the hill of faithfulness. The tribute He gives her is another example of the reversal of emphasis which takes place when the Tongue of Grandeur speaks on behalf of the receptive and reflective soul of man:

How piteous was her plight! In what a state of resignation she returned to her God! We, alone, in Our all-encompassing knowledge, have known it.[23]

The Unbroken Union

Finally, in the life of Navváb, the wife of Bahá'u'lláh and His 'perpetual consort in all the worlds of God',[24] we discover another facet of receptivity and one that most

* Ṭihrán

naturally evokes the imagery of the attendant cup-bearer, as well as the chosen beloved. For Navváb has been singled out among His handmaidens to serve Him, and has also been appointed 'the companion of His Person in the day-time and in the night-season'. But while she stands in attendance, she is being 'nourished . . . with His meeting and presence, so long as His Name, and His Remembrance, and His Kingdom, and His Empire shall endure.'[25] It is the eternal nature of this relationship which makes her the object of praise and emulation, for here no breach is possible, here can be no divorce. In her we find ourselves gazing at one whose life was an undivided gift, without separation between the conflicting demands of body and soul, the contrary tension between mind and heart. And, like her life, the Tablet Bahá'u'lláh reveals on her behalf, which confirms the eternal nature of this bond, does indeed 'gladden thine eye, and assure thy soul, and rejoice thine heart'.[26]

When we stand at the resting-place of Navváb and utter the words that Bahá'u'lláh has revealed on her behalf, it is as though we were praying that our lives too, like hers, might reflect a constancy and wholeness of response to the Greatest Name; that our certitude in the oneness underlying the sharp vicissitudes of this broken-surfaced world might never be shaken; that the seeming contraries within us might be reconciled and never be undermined; that we might lay hold on the cord of the Covenant with body and soul and heart and mind, and never suffer a breach to take place in all the worlds of God.

We might remember Navváb whenever we cannot quite succeed in combining the spiritual and material aspects of a Feast, for she succeeded in putting too much salt in a loaf of bread that somehow retains the sweet flavour of love in our remembrance; she somehow managed to wash the single shirt which Bahá'u'lláh owned during His exile from Írán while decking His precious Being with robes of honour and respect. And we might remember her too when our puritanical tendencies separate spiritual matters from physical ones; the Writings repeatedly exhort us to purity of motive, but do not summon us to God in sealed containers, certified with stamps of approval. The Cause invites us whole, but we would divide ourselves. The Revelation will not countenance schism, but all the habits of our minds tend towards partitioning. 'Abdu'l-Bahá calls upon us with all the vigour of His enthusiasm not to use our divisive mental instruments upon ourselves or the Cause of God: 'Let us not keep on forever with our fancies and illusions, with our analysing and interpreting and circulating of complex dubieties',[27] He says, for His hope is that we should recognize that our differences, like the seeming contradictions in the Cause, are 'the waves of one unending sea; for although blown about as the wind listeth, these are separate in themselves, yet in truth are they all at one with the boundless deep.'[28]

Once we have acknowledged this deep and boundless kinship we will not give undue emphasis to the differences between our separate understandings, and will know that it is our habits of mind which partition our response to the Cause:

O handmaid of God! Although the reality of Divinity is sanctified and boundless, the aims and needs of the creatures are restricted. God's grace is like the rain that cometh down from heaven: the water is not bounded by the limitations of form, yet on whatever place it poureth down, it taketh on limitations – dimensions, appearance, shape – according to the characteristics of that place . . . The rain itself hath no geometry, no limits, no form, but it taketh on one form or another, according to the restrictions of its vessel.[29]

The Revelation of Bahá'u'lláh, destined for every living soul, contains the contraries that surge within each living soul; yet it will not harbour any breach that would mar its subtle balance, for the health of the soul and civilization both depend on it. Having experienced the appalling nature of divorce between these contraries and wandered across deserts of dead response for however short a distance, we have surely learned to value the perfect harmony that Navváb symbolizes, and remember her station with a heartfelt prayer. And as we utter Bahá'u'lláh's mysterious words – words which so powerfully vindicate one who strove to remain faithful to the bond of trust and receptivity – it seems that their impact echoes to others, men and women, who might also address themselves to this challenge of whole-hearted response:

Happy is the handmaid that hath mentioned thee, and sought thy good pleasure, and humbled herself before thee, and held fast unto the cord of thy love. Woe betide him that denieth thy exalted station, and things ordained for thee from God, the Lord of all names, and him that hath turned away from thee, and rejected thy station before God, the Lord of the mighty throne.[30]

CHAPTER FOUR

The Power of Utterance

WE HAVE a tendency to confuse servitude with servility, and associate powerlessness with impotence. We sometimes assume that since silence has so much in common with passivity we should make free use of verbal energy to prove our thoughts and selves effective. Many of us pit ourselves against the conventional monotones of authority with a discord of claims in the upper range, and use our words like weapons. Indeed the tongue, that dubious instrument of vicarious power, has become our means to interpret the past to suit ourselves, to manipulate the present for personal gain, and to predetermine the future to our own advantage.

The world is full of voices. They are voices that whine, rail, flatter and appeal in order to wield what power they can. Words take revenge over submissive silence and prostitute themselves on all sides. Charging across the battlefields of advertising, they become impotent substitutes for the sword, that symbol of lost valour which once spoke with such sweeping and simple strokes of power. Is it any wonder then, that since we are so easily under the sway of spellbinders and gossip-mongers, personal charms and social complaint, Bahá'u'lláh exhorts us to turn to deeds. For listening can also be perverted, and language, used and abused by all, can lose its meaning: ' . . . words are the property of all alike, whereas such deeds as these belong only to Our loved ones.'[1]

It is sometimes hard for us to know where words end and actions begin in our dealings with each other. For a Faith without priests, some would say we have a tendency to sermonize (and that includes the present attempt!): priestcraft is a mentality and not merely a profession. Our willingness to offer advice and supply each other with maxims for successful living seems tireless. The very nature of our institutions, moreover, requires that decisions be implemented for a consultation to have been effective, and so when the cycle from words to deeds remains incomplete we may sometimes feel we have wasted our time, and may experience frustration without realizing why. For we feel the need strongly to exorcise the ancient witchery of equivocation – the deviation from responsibility for deeds – that can begin and end our lives in words that have no worth.

In the metaphorical universe Bahá'u'lláh has opened before our eyes, however, we discover that the faded language of the past has been transformed and every word has acquired a new and distinctive meaning. Action itself in this day has found its own praiseworthy voice, for work, according to Bahá'u'lláh, is also a form of worship, and service can become a form of prayer. Conversely, since speech and the power of utterance are, as we shall see, closely related to the sword – a traditional symbol of action – words, which are infused with the purpose of God for this day, become in the teaching field the highest form of endeavour.

A Double-Edged Sword

In the Writings of Bahá'u'lláh and 'Abdu'l-Bahá, the sword is an image which recurs with awesome frequency and deserves close attention in connection with a search for the speech of the spirit and the new language of resolution. Since so many veils, both literal and metaphorical, have shrouded our capacities to speak clearly about these matters, to use this symbol as a means of discovery and praise may not be inappropriate. For the tongue, like the sword, has the power to rend the curtain in the temple of our superstititions. It also has the power to tear the fabric of trust between souls. It has been endowed with the capacity both to murder and to create, and therefore needs to be masterfully commanded. When wielded in the name of God, 'the Almighty, the Unconstrained', the tongue can kindle the bushes, set the hearts ablaze, and cause the bodies to soar. When it is commanded by love it tears away the veils of superstition and shows us glimpses of true wisdom. When the cold metallic powers of the sword of self are plunged into the fire of the love of God, then

The qualities of the iron, its coldness, darkness and hardness are concealed, and it manifests heat, luminosity and fluidity, which are the qualities of the fire.[2]

So eloquence can rend the veils asunder, but sword-like it can also lacerate the heart, cause mortal wounds, and sever the ties that bind souls together:

For the tongue is a smouldering fire, and excess of speech a deadly poison. Material fire consumeth the body, whereas the fire of the tongue devoureth both heart and soul.[3]

Bahá'u'lláh warns us against the lethal powers of this

double-edged instrument of speech – 'he whose words
exceed his deeds, know verily his death is better than his
life'[4] – for the tongue, when used to backbite, to negate
and undermine, is committing a form of murder, which is
why 'The essence of true safety is to observe silence . . . '[5]
The tongue can all too easily become an instrument of
degradation and brutality, and, like the sword, can
butcher truth and botch the face of beauty. And we are
admonished in this respect: 'The tongue I have designed
for the mention of Me, defile it not with detraction.'[6]

In *Prayers and Meditations*, the image of the sword, which
literally becomes a threat to Bahá'u'lláh's very life, might
also be thought to refer to the calumniatory power of
speech which has been turned against Him and used to
desecrate the beauty of His Revelation. He calls upon God
to bear witness that 'Thou seest me sitting under a sword
hanging on a thread . . . ' and yet, despite this threat, He
seizes upon the sword of utterance Himself and wields it
with a power that would confound His enemies:

. . . in such a state I have not fallen short of my duty towards
Thy Cause, nor failed to shed abroad Thy praise, and declare
Thy virtues. . . . Though the sword be ready to fall on my head,
I call Thy loved ones with such a calling that the hearts are
carried away towards the horizon of Thy majesty and
grandeur[7]

Two Kinds of Power

It is significant, therefore, that clustered about the symbol
of the sword in the Bahá'í Writings, we find the connotations of two kinds of power: one that is illuminating,
exalting and expressive, and another that is quenching,
dominating, and destructive. The latter seeks to command

power by a self-assertion that incites force and coercion. The former implies that power, like the influence of human utterance, requires the timely response and a receptive atmosphere to be truly effective, and therefore cannot be said to control action, but rather to enable it to occur. If the motivation for power is not derived from the desire to reciprocate and collaborate in 'this glorious structure', then it is merely suppression. Authoritative power, like human utterance, 'is an essence which aspireth to exert its influence'.[8] Unless it is made sensitive to its responsibilities and conscious of the effects of its influence upon others, it will remain a primitive and dangerous tool, and, sheathed by our selfish motivations, we shall remain ignorant of its true worth, the artificer within us ignorant of our capacities.*

As if to waken us from our stagnant interpretations of power, Bahá'u'lláh's words overwhelm us with their unquestionable authority as He juxtaposes the new and old definitions of power through the image of the sword once more:

Say: The sword of wisdom is hotter than summer heat, and sharper than blades of steel, if ye do but understand. Draw it forth in My name and through the power of My might, and conquer, then, with it the cities of the hearts of them that have secluded themselves in the stronghold of their corrupt desires. Thus biddeth you the Pen of the All-Glorious, whilst seated beneath the swords of the wayward.[10]

The more evolved we become, therefore, as individuals

---

* 'The history of power struggles as we have known them has been on these grounds. The power of another person, or group of people, was generally seen as dangerous. You had to control them or they would control you. But in the realm of human development, this is not a valid formulation. Quite the reverse. In a basic sense, the greater the development of each individual the more able, more effective, and less needy of limiting or restricting others she or he will be.' (Jean Baker Miller)[9]

and through our social institutions, the more effective becomes our implementation of power in releasing the energies, inspiring the confidence, and actually enabling the souls around us to make effective use of their own powers. This is the principle governing the process of teaching the Cause. The Báb even creates a juxtaposition between the power released by teaching and that retained by an outdated concept of control: 'It is better to guide one soul than to possess all that is on earth . . . ' And He further clarifies the distinction between spiritual and material power when He asserts: 'The path to guidance is one of love and compassion, not of force and coercion. This hath been God's method in the past, and shall continue to be in the future!'[11]

We have identified power in contemporary society as something which controls action, and we have assumed that 'minorities' in the world have no freedom to act because of their powerlessness. It has become explicit in all terrorist campaigns and revolutionary activities that until people command power they cannot be in control of their own actions. But 'Abdu'l-Bahá seems to be indicating a different process that is both a reversal in the meaning of power and a change in the forms which action might take: ' . . . her actions will show her power,' He states, referring to women; 'there will no longer be any need to proclaim it by words.'[12] In a similar vein He affirms that 'Demonstrations of force . . . are neither becoming nor effective in the cause of womanhood and equality.[13] Finally, He clarifies what kind of power it is which needs neither words nor demonstrations of force to validate it: 'Women must make the greatest effort to acquire spiritual power and to increase in the virtue of wisdom and holiness until their enlightenment and striving succeeds in bringing about the unity of mankind.'[14]

It is probable that the power invested in the institutions of the Cause also shares this definition. Although authority rests in the Spiritual Assemblies, it is not dictatorial; although an individual's response needs to be tempered by obedience and respect, such attitudes cannot be produced on demand or nurtured in an atmosphere of administrative gossip. The immaturity of an Assembly does not indicate the insufficiency of the Administrative Order; one of its causes rests with the immaturity of individuals who have not yet acquired the response of a mother towards this infant institution. But the Assembly itself needs to discover the kind of power 'Abdu'l-Bahá associates with women: if it does not enlighten itself with the Writings which have been given to us for the healing of all ills, and strive to become fully cognizant of the problem it is undertaking to resolve, it cannot succeed in 'bringing about the unity of mankind'. The relationship between the individual and the Assembly is so conceived that when the latter is endowed with 'the virtue of wisdom and holiness' it will enable the former to make full use of his powers as a member of a growing community. 'Abdu'l-Bahá confirms, in a reference to the complementary dependence between men and women: 'As long as women are prevented from attaining their highest possibilities, so long will men be unable to achieve the greatness which might be theirs.'[15] It would appear that the same relationship is true of the response between Spiritual Assemblies and individuals, since the Writings stress that without the release and stimulation of individual initiative the finest decisions of the Assemblies will remain ineffective.

We, on the other hand, as individual Bahá'ís serving on these institutions, observing them from within the community, and teaching others about their significance, also need to strive and evolve beyond the rigid extremes to which our minds are habituated. Our aim is to discover the reconciliation in the Faith between the contraries of dominance and subservience, to which we are accustomed in relation to authority. The Administrative Order is neither a democracy in which we claim the right to make vociferous demands for individual freedom, nor is it an oligarchy which remains unrelated to our individual concerns in the community. Shoghi Effendi has, with an unerring hand, drawn the wide arc that links the varying points along the circumference of the Administrative Order, and shown us how it contains the best in each system of government and is protected from the extremes of each. The unique characteristic of this divine System, and the single element without which it could not effect this reconciliation, is that it is a fresh expression of humanity's response to the Covenant, couched in a language that has been taught to us by the Manifestation of God Himself. For the aim and motivation of this response is the integration of souls, the release of their potential, and the evolution of a spiritual as well as a material civilization. Far from limiting or diminishing the power in others, therefore, the Writings are inviting us to adopt a definition of power that increases our vital connections with other human beings, without the risk of exclusion. Like the power of speech, the implementation of social, political and economic power will be damaging and ineffective unless it be governed 'wholly for the sake of God and with due regard unto the exigencies of the occasion and the people.'[16]

The Unsheathed Soul

Power, then, in a Bahá'í context, is closely bound to progress in the spiritual worlds, for the effect of both power and utterance is 'conditional upon refinement which in turn is dependent upon hearts which are detached and pure'.[17] The connection between speech and power is clearly shown in Bahá'u'lláh's warnings in the *Hidden Words* against their negative use: 'Of all men the most negligent is he that disputeth idly and seeketh to advance himself over his brother.'[18] In the past, power has been used as a poor substitute for the spiritual qualities of collaboration, guidance, and nurturing of the mind and soul, but if we follow the metaphorical landmarks in the Writings we discover that the power of the sword has a vital role to play in revealing the uncharted country of the soul. For the sword, in the Writings of Bahá'u'lláh, symbolizes not only the tongue but also the spirit:

O My Servant! Thou art even as a finely tempered sword concealed in the darkness of its sheath and its value hidden from the artificer's knowledge. Wherefore come forth from the sheath of self and desire that thy worth may be made resplendent and manifest unto all the world.[19]

In meditating on the connotations of this metaphor we find ourselves actually employing the sword-as-utterance to discover the sword-as-soul. At no time are the Writings of this Revelation mere words, for they compel action from the moment they are uttered: having recognized the sword-like nature of language, we are drawn irresistibly to put it to use to part the enigmatic veils that conceal the reality of the soul. The attributes of the sword which seem to characterize the soul are several and fused together. The fire in which the blade is forged and strengthened is like the flame of love which burns away the veils that shroud the soul in this physical world, and through this heat the impurities of both are melted. Through such refinement the sword becomes a formidable force and cleaves through the seemingly solid elements of this material world, even as the soul, honed fine by suffering and desire, can penetrate and comprehend contingency. And finally, in relation to its Mighty Source, the swordlike soul can become a symbol of salute and obeisance, of recognition, submission, obedience and fealty to its Sovereign Lord.

It is the first among all created things to declare the excellence of its Creator, the first to recognize His glory, to cleave to His truth, and to bow down in adoration before Him.[20]

Since Bahá'u'lláh's words compel action it is not surprising to find that events in the history of the Cause best demonstrate this point.

The Active Force

There must have been countless unrecorded lives of those who did not speak, who chose to be choked rather than utter what they knew, but Bahá'u'lláh's Revelation has inaugurated a Day of exposition, of demonstration, of proofs. Gates stand wide and waiting, books are open and veils are drawn aside. Ṭáhirih, the martyr-poet of the Báb's Cause, is described by Shoghi Effendi as 'the noblest of her sex in that Dispensation,' and symbolizes above all the throat unlocked, the unseen beauty manifest, the most eloquent testimony to this new Revelation. We see her at the Conference of Badasht, 'a lone woman' standing upright as a flaming sword against the 'embattled forces of fanaticism, of priestcraft, of religious orthodoxy and superstition'. Paradoxically, in this scene the literal sword is held by Quddús, who symbolizes the 'conservative element' in the gathering, and who can barely restrain himself from striking her down in his fear and fury. Still more ironic is the fact that, although he wields the instrument of speech and authority, he is 'mute with rage', while she who has exposed her vulnerability to all, who has literally no premeditated power, commands certitude and joy.[21] 'I am the Word which the Qá'im is to utter, the Word which shall put to flight the chiefs and nobles of the earth!'[22] It is a moment so highly charged, so critical in Bahá'í history, that we cannot read Shoghi Effendi's words without a thrill of awe, for in this single action of Ṭáhirih we discover the resolution of so many symbols. In her personality we sense that the sheath has been removed from the tongue's fair sword, even as the bewilderment of self has been shed from her shining soul. The emblematic nature of this incident in Bahá'í history demonstrates for us that words need no longer be shimmering veils that cloak reality, that power depends upon the steadfast nature of perception, that we can begin to define the purposes of language and power neither by protest nor pretence, but by the naked eloquence of our spiritual understanding.

There may be moments in our own lives, whether we are men or women, when we would summon Ṭáhirih to our sides and tear veils in her name. Badas̲h̲t contains an awesome and timeless quality which we can conjure in the middle of a conversation, and encounter during a consultation at a Feast. But before we are tempted to raise the trumpet to our lips and expose the countenance of our concerns, we might remind ourselves of the most significant Participant in that event, Who Himself remained concealed throughout, within the tents of His wisdom. We need to ask ourselves if He has sanctioned our desires, for the power, the eloquence and the beauty of Ṭáhirih were at Bahá'u'lláh's command and not her own. The confrontation and reversal of roles at Bada<u>sh</u>t, while releasing a flood of bewilderment within everyone, was 'unerringly, yet unsuspectedly' directed by Bahá'u'lláh Himself, as Shoghi Effendi attests.[23] Every word that was uttered originated in His Will; even the identities of those present were transformed by His generative Pen and they became recipients of new names from that time. Is it any wonder, then, that the very Word itself, the 'irresistible' influence which is 'the Cause of the entire Creation',[24] the active force which traditionally belongs to our limited metaphorical concept of masculinity, was on this occasion symbolized by a woman? Ṭáhirih's audacity, impetuosity and fervour still have power to generate an upheaval within all who receive the impact of her announcement. Her eloquence becomes the instrument of the power of God, and revolutionizes our rigid formulations about this glorious structure.

It is also fascinating to see that Bahá'u'lláh Himself, at Bada<u>sh</u>t, uses the reversal of power to indicate the fresh definitions it has acquired in His Revelation, which emphasizes that the criteria of acceptance are recognition of and response to Him:

How many the veiled handmaidens who turned unto Me, and believed, and how numerous the wearers of the turban who were debarred from Me, and followed in the footsteps of bygone generations![25]

It is as a result of such reversals that we find our conventional formulae of power are shifting, for in the Writings, power is always defined in terms of one's relationship to God rather than to man; since we are all powerless before Him, our assumption of power over each other becomes ludicrous. Once we strengthen our relationship to God, and reconcile ourselves closely to this sense of powerlessness, the pull of contraries, the tug of competition is relieved. We begin to comprehend the 'sweetness of the title "O My handmaiden" ',[26] which 'Abdu'l-Bahá tells us

outshineth in glory the empresses of the world, for she is related to God, and her sovereignty is everlasting, whereas a handful of dust will obliterate the name and fame of those empresses.[27]

And finally, in the figure of Ṭáhirih, in the image of the sword, and in all reversals, we recognize symbols of that 'God-born Force' referred to by Shoghi Effendi, which with each age sweeps across the folds of society and ushers in with pain and triumph a new heaven and a new earth:

. . . such a Force, acting even as a two-edged sword, is, under our very eyes, sundering, on the one hand, the age-old ties which for centuries have held together the fabric of civilized society, and is unloosing, on the other, the bonds that still fetter the infant and as yet unemancipated Faith of Bahá'u'lláh.[28]

CHAPTER FIVE

BONDS

Praised be God that following the firm decree of separation, the breeze of nearness and communion hath been stirred and the soil of the heart is refreshed with the waters of joy and gladness.[1]

Bahá'u'lláh

IN *A Room of One's Own* Virginia Woolf writes that there is something yearning for the harmony of opposites in the mind, almost as though the mind itself were divided into male and female counterparts, which could only bear the tension of polarity for a certain time, and needed resolution. Perhaps this mental and spiritual conjunction is also implied in the passage quoted by 'Abdu'l-Bahá from the Qur'án, which states: 'Glory be to Him Who hath created all the pairs, of such things as earth produceth, and out of men themselves, and of things beyond their ken.'[2] The summoning of contraries to their fullest fusion, however, could not have been attained until this stage in the evolution of humankind. For we have been preoccupied until now in defining the contrasting and complementary capacities of the mind and soul; we have collectively been discovering piece by piece the nature of our 'true' selves. And in so doing we have been guided and educated by those divine Teachers without Whom we would not have been able truly to identify the contraries at work, or have known, through the juxtaposition of forces within ourselves, what principles and powers underlie this 'glorious structure' in which we move.

'Abdu'l-Bahá prompts this thought when He says:

The differences among the religions of the world are due to the varying types of minds. So long as the powers of the mind are various, it is certain that men's judgements and opinions will differ from one another.[3]

Becoming acquainted with the world of being and its jostling varieties has occupied us all in separate and apparently contradictory activities, but if, 'Abdu'l-Bahá continues, 'one single, universal perceptive power be introduced – a power encompassing all the rest – those differing opinions will merge, and a spiritual harmony and oneness will become apparent.'[4]

The Principle of Integration

Our business is to make bonds. All that tells us in this Faith of symmetry and harmony, confluence and order, penetrates our imaginations because of the energy of integration within it. Communication, whether tranquil or turbulent, which binds souls in spite of time or space, is the stuff of immortality, and we could no more cut ourselves loose of it than live without the co-ordinaton within our own bodies of blood and bone, breath and belief. All the exhortations against backbiting and calumny are rooted in this principle, for whatever is the cause of separation between deed and word, whatever breaks the tenuous fibres of trust between us, whatever interposes between ray and mirror, will result in our souls' decay. We cannot survive the lack of continuity in our lives on any level. To

break bonds of communication and response, therefore, is
a form of collective annihilation.

Annihilation is a process we usually apply to our bodies,
but it starts its lethal work on the thinking mind and keeps
the soul for its last tender morsel. What happens to the
body in between is a mere metaphor. Our fear of failure
and doubt in our capacities drives us into extraordinary
positions of attack and defence on the one hand, and
betrays us to utter self-abandonment on the other. It also
creates prejudice and distrust, for when no continuity
exists in our response between races and temperaments,
when we deny the validity of extension to our perpetually
evolving sense of truth, then we break the bonds between
us and spiritually die. 'Abdu'l-Bahá, in His capacity as
Exemplar for the Divine Physician of this age, warns us
against this deep disease of the soul, which is like a rejection of life after death:

> The conception of annihilation is a factor in human degra-
> dation, a cause of human debasement and lowliness, a source of
> human fear and abjection.[5]

There is not a great deal of difference between undermining the principle of integration within ourselves and
between each other and, according to 'Abdu'l-Bahá,
dwelling 'upon the thought of non-existence'[6], for while
the former negates the pattern of continuity in terms of
trust and friendship, the latter implies the same disintegration beyond the confines of the human world. In one,
the fabric of fellowship is torn between one soul and
another; in the other, the thread of communication is torn
between the soul and its Creator. And breaking such
bonds, in 'Abdu'l-Bahá's words, renders mankind 'utterly
incompetent'. When we lose trust in the communication of

truth at any level, we cut the veins of our will to survive in a spiritual sense, for doubt, fear and suspicion interpose, and like all who become subservient and are denied the freedom of the soul's expression, we suffer the fate of slaves: ' . . . with weakened will-power his ambition for progress will be lessened and the acquisition of human virtues will cease.'[7]

The maintaining of bonds and the nurturing of response has so beneficial an effect upon the health and strength of those in 'pairs' that, speaking about the lack of equality between men and women, 'Abdu'l-Bahá warns against a similar weakening of will and withering of spirit. He says that if collaboration between the sexes breaks down as a result of the 'assumption of superiority' by men, then 'woman's aspiration toward advancement will be checked by it and she will gradually become hopeless.'[8] It is significant that we find the same principle at work on a higher level in connection with the soul's response to its Creator. The annihilation of bonds as a result of man's withdrawal from this essential communication is a form of self-destruction: 'O Moving Form of Dust!' Bahá'u'lláh addresses us in our preoccupation amongst the world's 'divergent forms', 'I desire communion with thee, but thou wouldst put no trust in Me.'[9] The voice seems so near, so familiar, and we wonder momentarily why it should be that we ever find difficulty in trusting its Source. But in the next moment He tells us why: 'The sword of thy rebellion hath felled the tree of thy hope.'[9] There has been a sundering. The heart's seeds grow up always towards their Source of light and life, but we can with a moment's slur of certitude swing our unwieldy swords against the soul's very fibres and trail the leaves of our response and hope in mire and clay. That it should have been a tree, long in growing and supple in the winds of grace, which we so easily can fell with doubt's rebellion is the tragedy in the drama of response to God. That the heart's soil might yet prepare and purify itself to receive the countless seeds of hope still scattering remains the perpetual triumph.

It is curious how easily we are deluded by the superiority of doubt in our relationship with God. At its most extreme, in the form of Covenant-breaking, the superiority actually becomes an arrogance and our doubt becomes enough contaminated by the ego to assume we are our own Tree. The sundering is not simply a matter of broken communication then, but a complete loss of spiritual life; we are not only felling the supple trees of hope within ourselves that rise to greet the sun of Bahá'u'lláh, but are cutting ourselves off from the Tree of Life itself.

We are not concerned here with the extreme forms which severance from God can take, but rather with the daily doubts that trouble and separate us from people. The mire and clay from which doubt rises usually consist of fear and ignorance: fear of the unknown, and ignorance of the eternal patterns at work in the universe. We come across that fear in all kinds of lesser forms throughout our lives, and it is only knowledge of the greater and 'glorious structure' taught to us by the Manifestation of God that can dispel it. For the purposes of this book it might be sufficient to identify one of our fears as the fear of difference. The unknown nature of another human being may be enough to make us want to curl up against the back of our own indifference, or else hurl rejection at his face. It takes effort, especially in the Bahá'í community which can and should be so diverse, to apply the principles concerning prejudice and diversity to our everyday encounters with each other. But in case we imagine that it is only the saints who can effect such reconciliations – casting aside all fear and rushing forward towards certitude – Shoghi Effendi actually challenges the doubter to arise and test the truth of these principles. We have all experienced some form of doubt: doubt that we know enough about the Faith to teach it; doubt that the way we conduct the Feast at our home will be appreciated by the community; doubt that the Local Spiritual Assembly will be able to offer us the advice we need for a personal problem; doubt that we should pioneer, or marry, or study drama. The Guardian is not asking us to be magicians and send our doubts up in a puff of smoke. But he is calling upon us to come, doubts and all, and offer our broken, hesitant, and inadequate services to the Cause, for that is the road to certitude; that is the path from ignorance to knowledge; that is the beginning, perhaps, of the secret of mastering fear: 'Let the doubter arise and himself verify the truth of such assertions. To try, to persevere, is to insure ultimate and complete victory.'[10]

Vulnerability

It is an act of supreme vulnerability to be able to extend our arms outward in response, in spite of doubt. It is a gesture at once trusting and entirely free of expectation. It is the first step towards self-sacrifice, for we may assume that in the process we are losing something of our own identities. This threat surely challenges us when we read, once more, 'Abdu'l-Bahá's injunction to men, summoning them to enter an arena of extreme vulnerability in re-lationship to women. Far from assuming superiority over women, He suggests, 'On the contrary, we must declare that her capacity is equal to, even greater than man's.'[11]

How different is this gesture from that of withdrawal and fear which tears the frail bond of response between two different types and causes the withering of the soul! If individuals in a community, whose temperaments and cultures have kept them poles apart, were nevertheless able to respond to each other despite their sense of vulnerability, for the sake of their love for the Blessed Beauty, it would be a source of encouragement even as 'Abdu'l-Bahá's praise. For it surely takes more courage to reveal vulnerability than to exhibit the external trappings of mental or physical force. The individual, during a discussion, who is able to admit to being wrong, who asks for advice, who turns with gratitude towards an acknowledgement received, and offers suggestions in the spirit of a humility that admits to partial knowledge at best, surely evinces great courage indeed. And by such gestures of vulnerability others are greatly enriched, encouraged and lifted free above the contraries of attack and defence that would otherwise have caused a breach in communication.

In one of the Hidden Words which addresses the human race as 'O ye that are lying as dead on the couch of heedlessness!' Bahá'u'lláh describes a condition of arrogance and rejection that chills our hearts:

Him whom I abhor ye have loved, and of My foe ye have made a friend. Notwithstanding, ye walk on My earth complacent and self-satisfied, heedless that My earth is weary of you and everything within it shunneth you.[12]

From the Bahá'í Writings we know that the earth is a symbol of vulnerability and achieves the highest station of humility in the Kingdom of Names. We have Bahá'u'-

lláh's exhortation to us that we should strive to act in such wise that the earth may not turn to us and claim preference above us, since its 'absolute submissiveness' permits it to be 'trodden beneath the feet of men . . . '[13] In the Tablet of Visitation revealed by 'Abdu'l-Bahá we read that the greatest longing of His heart is to be 'as dust in the pathway of Thy loved ones'. And we know, too, that the soil of the human heart brings forth the fairest rose of love.

Might there not be a profound spiritual truth to be recognized in the subtle correlation between this symbol of humility, the earth, and that condition of sensitive response within our souls which, like the earth, accepts the outpouring of God's grace and the generative influence of the sun of His reality? Mankind's tendency to condense into solid form an imaginative response towards the great fluid patterns of the universe, pointed out to us by the prophets and messengers, has led to a literal interpretation of this relationship between the soul and God. Since the earth was traditionally associated with feminine qualities of fertility and procreation, as well as with the dark connotations of the underside of the psyche that remained unknown to us, we find a large body of literature accumulating across the centuries in which union with the Beloved is conceived in bridal terminology, in which virginity becomes a measure of the receptivity of the soul, and in which the concept of response and the integration of contraries is so literally conceived that there is no discrimination between the metaphors we are using to convey a spiritual message, and the *purpose* of that message. Exactly the same literalization has taken place, in the history of religion, with the concept of renewal and rebirth, which Bahá'u'lláh has described to us in spiritual terms, all the while maintaining the metaphors which we have known already. But we need to remember that the concept of response and integration in the relationship between the soul and its God is as different from the traditions we have accumulated about spiritual marriage as the concept of renewal or progressive revelation is from the literal interpretations of reincarnation and resurrection.

Protected from these extremities, therefore, we can turn and rediscover the Eve within our souls, who has for so many centuries suffered from a literal interpretation. For she is that instrument of receptivity within all of us, endowed with a capacity to accept and then impart 'unto all beings the blessings with which He Who is the Source of all grace hath entrusted Me'.[14] She is the 'feminine' response to the creative Word of God, the sensitivity with which we read, the openness with which we approach each other, the trust we have in our institutions, the humility which needs to attend our acts and words, the vulnerability with which we admit to partial understanding and incomplete knowledge of each other as well as of the mysteries of the Cause. Unless the Eve within is recognized, renamed and honoured, how can the bounties conferred upon us in this Revelation bear fruit in the continual advancement of civilization? How can the 'wealth that supplieth the needs of all creation'[15] be made evident in the quality of our individual lives, and in our relationships with one another?

It may increase our wonderment, as we explore the threads of connection between the responsive soul and the idea of this inner Eve, if we read 'Abdu'l-Bahá's interpretation of the symbol of Adam and Eve in *Some Answered Questions*, and also consider the following quotation with specific reference to the theme of this book:

'Adam' signifieth that reality which is pervasive, effulgent and active, that is the Manifestation of God's Names and Attributes, and the evidences of His mercy. Whereas 'Eve' is that reality which is the seeker and the recipient of the force, the grace, the message and the influence – that reality which receiveth the impact of all God's Names and Attributes.[16]

If woman, then, should be encouraged, according to 'Abdu'l-Bahá, and inspired 'with hope and ambition' so that 'her susceptibilities for advancement will continually increase',[17] how much more does the soul need encouragement in men and women alike, that its aspiration towards advancement might increase, its powers of receptivity and response be strengthened, and its vulnerability be perceived as courage which can in turn offer the sweet fruits of encouragement to other souls? It is to this end, therefore, that we are exhorted to forge bonds between us. It is these qualities of receptivity and response we develop between each other that nurture the human race towards its advancement. It is the homage we finally afford to that Eve within, sensitive to the influence of the Word of God, that enables us to reap the rich fruits of our lives. Only this homage can vindicate the spiritual reality inherent in the equality of men and women in this Day.

It is perhaps with the same purpose that 'Abdu'l-Bahá, in His *Memorials of the Faithful*, praises those souls who have arisen and exposed themselves to the incredulity of their countrymen, made themselves vulnerable to ridicule and scorn, and torn the chains of inhibition in order to forge the powerful bonds of love with the Cause. There are of course many levels of vulnerability. At one extreme, this can lead to martyrdom; at another, to the decision to allow meetings to take place in one's home. Bahá'u'lláh states in the *Hidden Words* that there are many ways in which our

commitment can be written on the tablet of our hearts –
with ink, blood, and the spirit of light – but the common
factor in all is that we allow ourselves to receive the
imprint of that symbol of love upon our souls. As in so
many circumstances of Bahá'í life, it is only the Divine
Assayer who can taste the pure beverage of sacrifice lifted
in our cupped lives. We can ourselves, at best, simply
judge by the shape and the design of the cup itself, which
tells nothing of the quality of inward commitment, the
vulnerability of devotion. It is in order to remind us of such
reversals that the Master so generously takes as an example one whose sacrifice we would not normally corre-
late with those great figures of martyrdom in Bahá'í
history, but whose vulnerability is as symbolic as theirs in
terms of relative sacrifice. 'Ponder and reflect how mighty
and potent hath the Cause of God become!' He writes in
triumph. 'A woman of the west hath given her hair for the
glory of the Mashriqu'l-Adhkár.'[18] It encourages these
souls who break from the bondage of self in order to forge
bonds of the spirit with each other and the Cause to read
that,

In this day there are women among the Bahá'ís who far out-
shine men. They are wise, talented, well-informed, progressive,
most intelligent and the light of men. They surpass men in
courage. When they speak in meetings, men listen with great
respect.[19]

Thus even in His comparison He simultaneously inte-
grates the roles of the two sexes and praises those who
recognize and listen, respect and respond to the courage of
the speakers. This surely is implicit in the magnificent
homage He offers women, for by announcing the manner
by which men will address them, He implies the station of

sensitivity and response, the parallel station of the powers of Eve within men themselves, when they will be able to say,

Blessed are ye! Blessed are ye! Verily ye are worthy of every gift. Verily ye deserve to adorn your heads with the crown of everlasting glory, because in sciences and arts, in virtues and perfections ye shall become equal to man, and as regards tenderness of heart and the abundance of mercy and sympathy ye are superior.[20]

Justice

It is difficult to give praise to another so long as we remain aloof and external to the living pulse of the one we praise. Once we identify the spiritual nature of another we shall recognize qualities that we ourselves may have in different measure, and then our praise comes from the heart's knowledge and bears tenderness towards the other. It is also difficult to testify to our own condition and capacities so long as we remain locked by internal vision and have not assessed our limitations in relation to a broader perspective that our own. Once we step out of a personal response to the Cause by recognizing some of the vast patterns of communication that apply to the whole human race, we are better able to bear witness to our potential and our purpose. Bahá'ís, therefore, are being called to both these challenges: we are being summoned to join the orchestra of the whole universe, and simultaneously sense the reverberation of the silent symphony within each others' souls. In everyday terms this means we have to learn to carry the magnitude and vision of the Cause into our humdrum affairs. We have to remember that, while we may hope to cover the points on the agenda, the Local

Spiritual Assembly is not effective in a community because of its efficiency but because of its sensitivity to reach and revive the growing spiritual lives of all whom it serves. It also means that we are not dividing our praise and encouragement amongst the believers to reach the different categories and minorities amongst us, but are addressing our respect and recognition to the spiritual nature within each other, the Eve within, whether we happen to be men or women, youth or children.

When 'Abdu'l-Bahá speaks of the equality of the sexes He says that the bird of humanity will not fly until 'both wings are reinforced with the same impulse'; until the same impulse motivates these contraries existent in the world, the bird will not be free 'to wing its flight heavenward to the summit of progress'.[21] Similarly, until we see with His eye and hear with His ear, we shall be unable to comprehend the message of Bahá'u'lláh. To be 'reinforced by the same impulse' seems to indicate that we need to be detached from a private and limiting perspective and at the same time intensely committed to a wider vision.

One of the reasons it may be difficult for us to appreciate fully 'Abdu'l-Bahá's phrase 'by the same impulse' could rest in our limited understanding of justice. Bahá'u'lláh states that justice is the 'best beloved of all things' in His sight,[22] but we sometimes make the mistake of inferring that objectivity, as the word is used today, is the same as justice. Our blind attachment to the 'criteria of objective judgment' may sometimes cause us actually to avoid the responsibility of seeing with our own eyes for fear of being 'subjective' – a word that has become loaded with negative connotations. As a result we may observe the world and the reality of the Cause of God according to the 'objective' standards set by other people's eyes, and thus remain entirely deprived of His gift.

Justice is a form of objectivity which has as its goal a more accurate measure and experience of circumstances in relation to the standards established by the Cause of Bahá'u'lláh. And one of these standards is empathy. How often in the Writings we find ourselves summoned to be 'a refuge to the fearful . . . rest and peace to the disturbed . . .'[23] We are told, 'Beware lest ye harm any soul, or make any heart to sorrow; lest ye wound any man with your words, be he known to you or a stranger, be he friend or foe.'[24] We are urged to keep our fingers on the pulse of all about us, on their joys and their distress, their doubt and their delusions, that we may more accurately prescribe for them the remedy of all ills in this Day. And in our response to the Cause of God there can be no rational restraint admitted as we burn ourselves like candles and scorch ourselves like moths. 'Abdu'l-Bahá's pen seizes upon our reluctant cautions and flings our 'standards of objective judgment' to the winds of God:

Even as the clouds let us shed down tears, and as the lightning flashes let us laugh at our coursings through east and west.[25]

Indeed, the criterion which Bahá'u'lláh establishes for approach to Him is that we should not, at any cost, do it 'with lifeless hearts'.[26] The quality that makes us worthy to meet Him is not our detachment, or the smooth control we bring to bear upon our relationships with others, or even the precision of our analyses about our weaknesses or limitations, but simply the degree to which we are able to commit ourselves wholly to the sheer joy of meeting Him:

O Son of Man! Rejoice in the gladness of thine heart, that thou mayest be worthy to meet Me and to mirror forth My beauty.[27]

However, the intensity of our response has nothing to do with the extravagance of its expression, any more than true justice has much to do with technical objectivity. Both these are external masks of an internal condition, and the challenge to feel the 'same impulse' is directed to the heart of mankind and not to manifestations of social gesture, which in their varying expressions might be either intellectual postures or political grimaces. Bahá'u'lláh is not directing the intensity of His gaze to our performance in the theatre of social acceptability. He has His eyes fixed deeply within, and the quality of our response to such a gaze must surely match it in intensity, however limited our capacity:

It is not Our wish to lay hands on your kingdoms [He addresses the kings]. Our mission is to seize and possess the hearts of men. Upon them the eyes of Bahá are fastened. To this testifieth the Kingdom of Names, could ye but comprehend it.[28]

It is the depth and penetration of this steady gaze to the very centre of our beings that can bring us to the equilibrium of 'the Middle Way'; this is the resolution that we crave. For by 'the remembrance of Me in your afflictions and reflection over that which may befall you in future',[29] we are able to compare our tribulations to His which were so much worse, and to consider the bounties by which we are surrounded and which may not always be our lot. Bahá'u'lláh's injunction, 'Lament not in your hours of trial, neither rejoice therein',[30] teaches us something of that condition of tranquillity so beautifully evinced in the life of the Greatest Holy Leaf.

It is in the portrait exquisitely penned by Shoghi Effendi that we find this resolution of extremes depicted by her life, a resolution that must evolve from the integrating insight of 'the wise souls who are aware of the essential relationships emanating from the realities of things . . .'[31] And perhaps it is a measure of the potency endowed in such spiritual resolutions that neither time nor space, death nor division can cloud the beauty of the Greatest Holy Leaf:

Through the mist of tears that fill my eyes I can clearly see, as I pen these lines, thy noble figure before me, and can recognize the serenity of thy kindly face. I can still gaze, though the shadows of the grave separate us, into thy blue, love-deep eyes, and can feel in its calm intensity, the immense love thou didst bear for the Cause of thine Almighty Father, the attachment that bound thee to the most lowly and insignificant among its followers, the warm affection thou didst cherish for me in thine heart.[32]

This quality of 'calm intensity' is paralleled in the manner and quality of Ṭáhirih's speech at Badasht where, according to the powerful description of Shoghi Effendi, Ṭáhirih arose 'undeterred, unruffled, exultant with joy'.[33] Such a combination of detachment and fervour surely establishes the standard of ideal communication between souls and must necessarily be the only type of resolution possible between the wrangling contraries within ourselves.

Ideal Communication

'Abdu'l-Bahá tells us that He is 'constantly engaged in ideal communication' with any Spiritual Assembly which is firm in the Covenant. The degree of total commitment and participation He anticipates with such an Assembly is conveyed by His assertion:

To them he is whole-heartedly attached and with them he is linked by everlasting ties. Thus correspondence with that gathering is sincere, constant and uninterrupted.[34]

This invites us to conceive of an intensity of communication that is generally unavailable to us, and is almost incredible to the majority of us. In spite of the plethora of words expended on the need for communication in our modern world, it is very rare for us to maintain such sincere, constant response with one another. Neither in our work nor, for the most part, in our marriages; neither between the contradictions we carry around inside ourselves nor among those which jostle in our lives, have we discovered a sustained and vital thread of connection that will not break down under the strain of communication.

Perhaps because the desire for resolution is so deep and so intense, we find ourselves imitating ideal communication. We have invented languages that pretend at synchronization; we simulate the simultaniety of impulse. We even read books and take courses on how to convey the impression of genuine concern. But so often we never touch the tingling stars within each others' souls as such a reaching love would promise to. We crave the marriage between word and heart, but often find we lack the courage of commitment to convey it truly. We sometimes imitate its voice, perch on the brittle parrot-cage of choice, and trill the language of sincerity. But something in the heart may well remain unsolaced. And so often disappointed we may hesitate to try again, and say it cannot be achieved. It can seem an ideal that is beyond our reach:

. . . when any souls grow to be true believers, they will attain a spiritual relationship with one another, and show forth a tenderness which is not of this world. They will, all of them, become elated from a draught of divine love, and that union of theirs, that connection, will also abide forever.[35]

It is because we have all, at some level in our lives, dreamed or experienced this communication 'from heart to heart'[36] that we yearn to repeat it. It is because we experience such profound fulfilment from our response to the Covenant that we strive to emulate it in our lesser relationships and 'the close and intimate association'[37] of souls on this plane. 'Abdu'l-Bahá informs us that 'In every century a particular and central theme is, in accordance with the requirements of that century, confirmed', and adds that 'In this illumined age that which is confirmed is the oneness of the world of humanity.'[38] We are so committed to this ideal that we long for the time when 'all nations will mingle one with another, dealing with one another even as the lover with his beloved'.[39] This would surely bring with it a harmony of contraries within the mind that we have assumed to be a lost utopian ideal.

But 'Abdu'l-Bahá did not tell us only of the ideal; He also assured us that we could attain it:

Perchance thou deemest this to be difficult, but I tell thee that such cannot be the case, for when the motivating and guiding power is the divine force of magnetism it is possible, by its aid, to traverse time and space easily and swiftly.[40]

To traverse time and space lies at the kernel of our soul's desire to speak. That is the very longing that involved us in this search. With the doors of access to Him flung wide, we find ourselves in huddled wonderment, invited to step inside 'this glorious structure' and see for the first time the complementary beauty of His designs. We wander about, inarticulate, and lift our heads in awe to gaze and see how high indeed are flung the arches, how smooth and sure the

pillars stand, how the sweet dome rises to greet the Divine
Architect's desire for utter harmony. And so to span these
spaces we too would learn to use our complementary
powers. Through consultation and solitary prayer, by
collaboration and initiative, we would build high with
ever more evolved designs. We long to construct edifices of
an architectural beauty and spiritual complexity that no
civilization has attained before us, because of these newly
defined laws of complementary harmony between the
contraries, upon which our lives must swing:

Walk thou high above the world of being through the power of
the Most Great Name, that thou mayest become aware of the
immemorial mysteries and be acquainted with that wherewith
no one is acquainted. Verily, thy Lord is the Helper, the All-
Knowing, the All-Informed. Be thou as a throbbing artery,
pulsating in the body of the entire creation, that through the
heat generated by this motion there may appear that which will
quicken the hearts of those who hesitate.[41]

Resolution

There are two forms which resolution must take; both are
implied in this quotation of Bahá'u'lláh, and both are
symbolic of the subtle differences in the complementary
natures of the contraries we are resolving. The first form
relates to that structure of marvellous balance which raises
the framework on which we might 'walk high'. This is in
simplest terms the Administrative Order, with its clear
connections, its patterns of institutions, its assemblies that
enable the individual to step above personal limitations
through submission to and collaboration with the community. The second form is an inward attitude, which, like
the vital arteries in the body of mankind, kindles a spiri-

tual life within this structure that binds us to its Source through the pulse of the Covenant. It is the harmonious merging of these two – the outer framework and the inner heat – that sets 'hearts of true believers ablaze and cause[s] their bodies to soar',[42] which enables the balance and beauty of the Administrative Order to flow with life. The two aspects of resolution are inextricably bound together: both rest upon the implementation of response between the contraries in our minds; both find their fulfilment in the World Order of Bahá'u'lláh.

Since we have been using language itself as a metaphor by which we might discover the resolution of these contraries, it becomes clear, as we read the Writings, that the two aspects of resolution indicated above also find themselves two distinctive and complementary forms of language. We have already found that there is a very high standard set for communication, but, like inextricably bound 'pairs' that provide the framework for ' this glorious structure', language too can take on two forms of expression which are the same, yet also different.[43] The first, relating to the external structure of the Administrative Order, is the language of consultation. The second, which gives expression to the 'heat' mentioned in the previous quotation, is the language of compassion, that twin luminary by which 'the heaven of divine wisdom is illumined'.[44]

These two forms of ideal communication together lead to the culmination of the potentialities inherent in the original equation between ear and tongue. They also symbolize the conflation of influences necessary for the ultimate birth of a new world order 'now stirring in the womb of a travailing age'.[45] For Shoghi Effendi clearly identifies the complementary 'male' and 'female' principles at work in the emergent Administrative Order itself, which must interact upon the spirit and society of man in order to generate a heat by whose motion 'there may appear that which will quicken the hearts of those who hesitate'.[46] In *God Passes By* he gives us an awe-inspiring glimpse of the profound implications of the 'active' and 'recipient' forces at work, from the world of matter onward through the mysterious cycles of the spirit:

The Covenant of Bahá'u'lláh had been instituted solely through the direct operation of His Will and purpose. The Will and Testament of 'Abdu'l-Bahá, on the other hand, may be regarded as the offspring resulting from the mystic intercourse between Him Who had generated the forces of a God-given Faith and One Who had been made its sole Interpreter and was recognized as its perfect Exemplar.[47]

The complementary roles enacted by Bahá'u'lláh and 'Abdu'l-Bahá in relation to the Instrument of World Order illuminate for us our own insignificant yet integral part in the majestic process at work around us.

To the extent that we have committed our energies to the evolution of this Administrative Order, to the degree to which we have learnt to articulate the twin languages of consultation and compassion, we too are affected, transformed, and renewed in our individual lives and within our institutions. For Bahá'u'lláh exhorts us repeatedly to commit ourselves through deeds and purify our words, and the degree to which we can achieve either of these obligations depends upon our slow, groping comprehension of the subtle interrelationships of complementary roles within this Revelation itself:

The creative energies unleashed by the Originator of the Law of God in this age gave birth, through their impact upon the mind of Him Who had been chosen as its unerring Expounder, to that Instrument, the vast implications of which the present generation . . . is still incapable of fully apprehending.[48]

CHAPTER SIX

Compassion and Consultation

Vision and Form

We are preoccupied with the need to discover a fit form for our visions. Whether we are conscious of it or not, throughout our lives each attempt to find a career, or to choose the readings for a Feast, to raise a child, or to proclaim the Faith, is a different variation on the same theme. For if our response to life and to the Faith is intense, as it must be if we are to be more than spiritual corpses, then we are driven through calm and tempest to find the clearest and most congruent outward expression of the flame within.

Similarly, it would seem that our greatest misery occurs when the outward form fails to be an adequate vehicle for the blaze of our vision. Our frustrations in our marriages, the tensions in our communities, the difficulties we have as individual Bahá'ís in conforming our lives to the Teachings, stem from the flawed relationship between our outer acts and the inner spirit of faith which yearns to find a fit expression for itself. Our despair and anger are motivated by the divorce between form and spirit; our highest expectations and most destructive cynicism spring from the dichotomy between them. And each time we speak of love, or lean in friendship, or learn a new language of the spirit, it is that we might once again arrive at a more comprehensive resolution, at a more fit and perfect form to frame our ideals.

But how are we to accomodate to our inevitable failures? If we are to avoid the pitfalls of 'the concept of annihilation', with its fiercely restricted perspective that so undermines the continuity of hope within us, the birds of our hearts need something to sustain their fluttering wings, some azure assurance that would make the effort of striving worthwhile. If we should focus only on the evidences of decay and dissolution round us, and address ourselves only to what appears to be an infinite variety of failures, whether in political systems or in cancer research, we should have less than a world-embracing vision indeed. We should not have gone on the round trip that recognizes birth in decay. We should have ignored 'Abdu'l-Bahá's salient point that 'whensoever a thing is destroyed, and decayeth, and is cut off from life, it is promoted into a world that is greater than the world it knew before.'[1] The process of dissolution of one form into another, as our vision moves from stage to stage, is similar to the decay of living organisms and is to be expected, for it is 'the very fabric of life'. 'Were it not so,' 'Abdu'l-Bahá assures us, 'the ties that interlace all created things within the universe would be unravelled.'[2]

Failure, then, should not surprise us, any more than death need grieve us. If we can read the words of 'Abdu'l-Bahá aright, we may begin to see that loss is not a deprivation of hope but a lack of perspective. 'Reflect upon the inner realities of the universe,' He tells us, the secret wisdoms involved, the enigmas, the inter-relationships, the rules that govern all. For every part of the universe is connected with every other part by ties that are very powerful and admit of no imbalance, nor any slackening whatever.[3]

Indeed, to perceive the lack of harmony between structure and spirit as failure is to remain veiled from the well-guarded mystery and hidden secret of progressive revelation, by which we learn that knowledge of the laws of integration that govern the universe has been taught to us in stages, and that we must necessarily move from one structure to another in both art and scientific knowledge, as we discover more about the 'glorious structure' underlying all. Since all things 'are subject to transformation and change', belief too will move 'past one barrier after another'[4] as we explore, cell by cell, the changeless religion of God. Shoghi Effendi confirms this organic development of religious formulae when he writes:

Why should these, in a world subject to the immutable law of change and decay, be exempt from the deterioration that must needs overtake every human institution?[5]

As we grow in our comprehension of this endless flux and ceaseless motion from form to form, we also become cognizant, through the frail film of living things, of the steady and undeviating force of 'the Cause of existence itself – since He is constant and immutable, and upon Him is founded the existence of every species and kind, of every contingent reality throughout the whole of creation.'[6] In our search for a spiritual language commensurate with the needs of this age, we need to discover a form that recognizes the evolutionary aspects of life as well as its 'ancient, imperishable and everlasting'[7] Cause. What imperishable structure, therefore, can we find that lends itself to this very principle of transformation? What everlasting language can we adopt that has enfolded within itself the priority of revealing rather than restricting truth, as our relative understanding of it evolves? What eternal marriage between contraries could we conceive that forges bonds which do not become bondage between us?

Twin Languages

We discover in the Writings of the Bahá'í Faith that there are two languages which, woven together, create a tapestry rich and fair on which to couch response to the Covenant. While the individual rainbow threads are familiar to us, the manner in which they have been interlaced, each lending strength and beauty to the whole, is unique and will take centuries to trace. And as we caress this shimmering fabric of the Cause we know that we can never unravel the two interwoven threads from each other in our attempts to understand. The Powers that spun them are beyond our fingering minds, and we but cling to the hem of what we hold.

The first language primarily concerns the individual and his expression of service, and could be called the language of compassion, a thread of fine gold that carries the arterial fire of inspiration and intimate communication from soul to soul. The second might be called the language of consultation, and is the expression of collaboration in groups, the voice of justice and authority, a thread of luminous whiteness, of transparent strength, of complementary powers against whose symmetry the single soul weaves his exquisite patterns. The language of compassion is that which sets 'the hearts of true believers ablaze and cause[s] their bodies to soar';[8] it is the language used by the individual to 'quicken the hearts of those who hesitate';[9] it is the language, at times, of teaching. The language of consultation is that used by the Assemblies and Institutions of the Administrative Order: it is the language of definition and decision; it is the language of order and collaboration necessary for the flowering of civilization. The complete harmony between the two languages is obvious from the fact that individuals are exhorted to consult at all times, and institutions are exhorted to concentrate on teaching. The distinction between them, and the need for us to discover the complementary functions they perform, are demonstrated by Shoghi Effendi when he reminds us, through his secretary, of the difference of tone between the communication used by Assemblies and that used by individuals:

There is a tendency to mix up the functions of the Administration and try to apply it in individual relationships, which is abortive, because the Assembly is a nascent House of Justice and is supposed to administer, according to the Teachings, the affairs of the community. But individuals toward each other are governed by love, unity, forgiveness and a sin-covering eye. Once the friends grasp this they will get along much better, but they keep playing Spiritual Assembly to each other and expect the Assembly to behave like an individual . . .[10]

The fact that we need two complementary languages tells us as much about the flexibility and comprehensive nature of the Cause as it does about the inherent laws that protect it from the corruption of man's limiting imagination. In the *Lawh-i-Maqṣúd* Bahá'u'lláh identifies the twin luminaries of consultation and compassion, of tolerance and righteousness, of consummate learning and penetrating wisdom. Within each of these pairs can be found the paradoxes that have dominated our civilizations, our art, our temperaments throughout history. Here is the marriage between mercy and justice, between art and instruction, between the free will of the individual and his submission to the best interests of the group. And Bahá'u'lláh admonishes us not to fall into the restricting arguments of comparison, for He stresses that these pairs are as 'two eyes to the body of Mankind', the lights in 'the heaven of true understanding', and the luminaries in 'the heaven of divine wisdom'.[11] Like the marriage between a man and a woman, these two languages of compassion and consultation are two bright orbs 'wedded in Thy love, conjoined in servitude to Thy Holy Threshold, united in ministering to Thy Cause.'[12] When these twin luminaries rise with equal brightness on our horizons, we may perhaps convey something of the truth of the Cause in the way we communicate our lives to others:

Their outward conduct is but a reflection of their inward life, and their inward life a mirror of their outward conduct. No veil hideth or obscureth the verities on which their Faith is established.[13]

We see, from the passage quoted above, that the characteristic shared by both languages is best described by metaphors of lamps – structures through which the light streams unimpeded. The aim of our individual and collective lives, it would seem, is to become a source of illumination, and we know enough about the imagery of mirrors and rays of sunlight to realize that the only way this can happen is to strive to turn whole-heartedly and respond to the light of the Revelation. Both languages, therefore, convey the light and heat of the Cause across this darkened world, and the difference between them will be explored in the following pages and described in terms that relate first to the individual voice and, secondly, to the voice of the Assemblies and Institutions of the Administrative Order.

Compassion and the Individual

Throughout the Writings of Bahá'u'lláh we discover ourselves referred to as lamps, as lights, as candles lit by His love. 'Thou art My lamp' He says, 'and My light is in thee. Get thou from it thy radiance and seek none other than Me.'[14] And again He urges, 'Thou art My light and My light shall never be extinguished, why dost thou dread extinction?'[15] He hails us with 'the joyful tidings of light'[16] and assures us that 'My light is manifest to thee, it cannot be obscured.'[17]

A lamp not only contains light but conveys it too. It has an outer form transparent enough to express its inner worth; it is the message and the messenger. But the condition of transparency, symbolized by the lamp, lends itself easily in the eyes of a perverse and hypocritical society as something to be abused and ridiculed. For a person to mean what he says, to keep his promise, and strive to be trustworthy, is almost laughable, according to contemporary standards. We are more likely to be trying to convince someone of our sincerity than striving toward it ourselves. It is often assumed that 'extenuating circumstances' will absolve us from the pressure of a promise, and trust is sometimes more of an embarrassment than an aspiration. We are better acquainted with the causes that cloud honesty and candour than with the spiritual necessity to nurture such qualities. Indeed, transparency is so naive an attribute that we are less proud to be guiltless than to demonstrate our guile.

And yet, according to the Teachers of the divine art of reading, there can be no doubt that unless we are able to combine 'holy words' with 'pure and goodly deeds'[18] we have sadly misconstrued the purpose of the language of the spirit we have been learning. For the fruit of all utterance is action; the resolution of all verbal paradox lies in the quality of our daily lives. To demonstrate the effects of this spiritual language, we are told by 'Abdu'l-Bahá that we should 'live and move according to the Divine commands and behests . . .'[19] This, in fact, is His definition of the word 'striving'. And the Writings call upon us ceaselessly to strive, to move, to seek no rest, to arise, to turn and return towards Bahá'u'lláh's guidance and His laws. The action implicit in the word 'striving' seems to tell us that our responsibility lies precisely in this ability to yearn, aspire, and endeavour again and again to conform our lives to Divine commands and behests.

It is only when we conform the nature of our deeds to the quality of our words that we may vindicate the value of the spiritual language in the world. And since the stuff of immortality is to forge bonds one with another, to strengthen the principle of integration within society and the subtle patterns of communication between all created things, we can appreciate why the language of compassion should have been referred to by Bahá'u'lláh as a luminary through which the beams of His tenderness and warmth might shine from heart to heart.

Compassion is a quality that conveys heartfelt concerns as well as perceives them in another person. It is a language that requires a transparency of response in both speaker and spoken-to, and it has no special vocabulary. It is not conveyed through a well-turned phrase, but in spite of it. It resides as much in the silence we share as in the words we use. The language of compassion enables us to express the unspoken, for by its aid we lean closer than the words themselves allow, and touch chords of response in the hearer that echo in the privacy of inner chambers. Like prayer, the language of compassion reverberates through the veil of words and past the clumsiness of deeds to cause 'the heart of every righteous man to throb.'[20]

Since it can take on a myriad different forms, the language of compassion lies waiting for us in a myriad different places too, most of them unannounced and unprepared. We may be anywhere, with anyone, and all the world be tumbling around us, but however unpremeditated are the circumstances, compassionate response between two stranger souls takes us to a place we cannot but recall – 'beneath the shade of the tree of life, which is planted in the all-glorious paradise'.[21] By what miracle of faith did we remove so silently, from a simple conversation, from a gesture, from a pause, to this familiar landscape? What magic lingers in our words that makes them prayers, that takes them past their fragments and their flaws and quietly relates them to the beauty of Bahá'u'lláh? The words we uttered were born simply enough but, cradled by compassionate response, we are enabled to stand and listen awestruck to His Voice within our hearts.

'Abdu'l-Bahá tells us that when 'man's soul is rarified and cleansed, spiritual links are established'.[22] These links recall our absolute equality and mutual powerlessness before the Will of God. Through them we respect each other's sincere efforts to abide by that Will, and appreciate the contrary poles upon whose axis our souls revolve. How can we not feel bound together? How can we gaze at one another without strange wonder stirring? We cannot speak without our hearts rising like birds in greeting. A tenderness which is not of this world sings unspoken in our throats, and all the differences of temperament and personality, of culture and accomplishment, must melt in the heat of this unparalleled emotion. And so 'Abdu'l-Bahá confirms:

. . . from these bonds sensations felt by the heart are produced. The human heart resembleth a mirror. When this is purified human hearts are attuned and reflect one another, and thus spiritual emotions are generated.[23]

It is with a refreshed and vivid apprehension that we now read Bahá'u'lláh's promises concerning the effects of teaching on the soul:

O Friends! You must all be so ablaze in this day with the fire of the love of God that the heat thereof may be manifest in all your veins, your limbs and members of your body, and the peoples of the world may be ignited by this heat and turn to the horizon of the Beloved.[24]

And the words of the Báb reinforce our understanding:

It is better to guide one soul than to possess all that is on earth, for as long as that guided soul is under the shadow of the Tree of Divine Unity, he and the one who hath guided him will both be recipients of God's tender mercy . . .[25]

Since the station of the recipient of God's grace is so highly praised in this Day, is it any wonder that teaching the Cause is the most meritorious of all deeds? Or that we realize with no surprise that we ourselves are enkindled when we teach? For through such throbbing arteries of communication 'pulsating in the body of the entire creation',[26] we are told, the heat of spiritual response to the Covenant is generated. If, then, we can 'be kindled with the fire of His love', if by that refinement of our hearts we can forgo 'all created things', then, according to Bahá'u'lláh, the words we utter 'shall set on fire them that hear . . .'[27] Our language will become the echo of the blaze and the roar of the Fire 'which Thou didst kindle in Thy land'.[28] Neither the doubts of the earth nor the vacillations of our thoughts will quench or cloud the potency of the message we bear on our lips. If we draw near to this Fire ourselves and are thus blessed, we shall take on the attributes of this intense language heard in 'the heaven of communion with Me',[29] and shall be able to teach 'with an utterance which will cause the bushes to be enkindled, and the call "Verily, no God is there but Me, the Almighty, the Unconstrained" to be raised therefrom.'[30]

There can be no sweeter consummation, in our attempts to enter into communication with a God 'who settest my soul on fire',[31] than to find ourselves the candles, the lamps, the burning brands that carry this intensity into a darkened world and draw humanity towards it:

Thy glory beareth me witness, O Thou, the Light of the world! The fire of Thy love that burneth continually within me hath so inflamed me that whoever among Thy creatures approacheth me, and inclineth his inner ear towards me, cannot fail to hear its raging within each of my veins.[32]

And as we realize the privilege of this communication, we discover, in the language which Bahá'u'lláh has taught us, our sweetest form of response, that of gratitude and praise: 'I render Thee thanks, O Thou Who hast lighted Thy fire within my soul, and cast the beams of Thy light into my heart . . .'[33]

The lamp of an individual soul, however, can be shrouded by veils and choked by dust. Its transparency can be clouded by 'the contrary winds of self and passion'.[34] Though our hearts have been 'lighted by the hand of My power',[35] the turbulence of these contraries within us can easily quench them. Language which expresses individual perception and desire can also be tainted by 'the dust of self and hypocrisy',[36] so that when we respond to the Cause our words and actions themselves may interpose veils between the beauty of Bahá'u'lláh and others:

O Dwellers in the City of Love! Mortal blasts have beset the everlasting candle, and the beauty of the celestial Youth is veiled in the darkness of dust.[37]

It is obvious, therefore, that while individuals can be set alight by the truth of the Cause and become candles of commitment and torches of fidelity, nevertheless there are also 'lamps of error' wavering through these marshy ways. Mesmerized by false lights, we can lose our path and wander straying, the radiance of our hearts turned 'into infernal fire'.[38] Indeed, each individual lantern is so weak, so feeble, so subject to limitation and failure, that we are entirely fallible even when we inscribe the letters of our faith 'with the ink of light upon the tablet' of our spirit.[39]

Consultation and the Spiritual Assembly

It is because of this fallibility and frailty of the individual flame, this tarnishable quality of our personal expressions in response to the Cause, that we find a ring of bright lights about the Covenant, a constellation of Spiritual Assemblies that circle the flame of this Revelation with a constancy of glass. While we may strive and fail and strive again through crisis and victory to grope our way as individuals towards our Beloved, the transparency of the institutions of the Cause enables its inner spirit to be conveyed in action with a more steady flame. Knowing full well our frailties, Bahá'u'lláh does not abandon us to the perilous inconsistencies of a world whose defilement can so easily eclipse our individual splendour.[40] Instead, He alerts us to a majestic process which began six thousand years ago, and has for centuries been evolving, that we might now for the first time celebrate its consummation. It is a process which Shoghi Effendi describes through the imagery of the light and the lamp, so that we realize the exquisite harmony achieved between the spirit and the form. And since the process crosses steppe-lands of slow development, we are given a fleeting glimpse from a divine perspective, without which neither purpose nor harmony would be apparent.

In his *Messages to the Bahá'í World* Shoghi Effendi describes the 'slow and steady growth' of the 'tree of divine revelation', to the point where it bore its sacred fruit in the person of the Báb. The persecution which befell Him is likened to 'the grinding of this sacred seed, of infinite preciousness and potency, in the mill of adversity, causing it to yield its oil' in His martyrdom. This oil was soon ignited 'in the depths and amidst the darkness' of the dungeon of the Síyáh-Chál, where Bahá'u'lláh received the first intimation of His Revelation. Then, after being clothed in the 'lamp of revelation' in Baghdád, this light gradually spread its radiance through the crystal globe of His revealed Covenant, across oceans and seas, and is destined to penetrate 'all the remaining territories of the globe through the erection of the entire machinery of Bahá'u'lláh's Administrative Order in all territories, both East and West . . .'[41]

The level beam of light that gleams through this description across the random motions of darkness offers us a perspective and illuminates the past and future with such unparalleled clarity that we may well be left breathless when we compare our individual flickerings of insight with the steady illumination cast by the institutions of the Cause. For the Administrative Order, in this age, is not only the lamp but the temple of light through which all lamps can shine. The institutions of the Faith are not simply an assortment of torches and candles, but the altars, beacons and tabernacles from whence the sweet rays spread far and wide.

For an individual who is the lamp in which the light and radiance of the Faith have found their home, the language which best lends itself to a reflection of that inner spirit is that of teaching. By conveying the essential verities of the Faith to another soul with the power of eloquence, the wisdom of self-restraint, complete detachment, and an intense sensitivity to the quality of response, a Bahá'í is able to unite all contraries and be both the active force and its recipient. At the very moment he is teaching the Cause, he will also be learning from its life-giving message, from the reactions of the one he is teaching, and from his own failures to be a pure and translucent lamp through which the radiance of the Cause may fitly shine.

For an institution, on the other hand, which is the 'shining mansion' in which the altar of our commitment burns, the the highest form of expression is the language of consultation. Shoghi Effendi confirms that this must be the language which conveys the collective interests of the Faith because

Individual initiative, personal ability and resourcefulness, though indispensable, are, unless supported and enriched by the collective experiences and wisdom of the group, utterly incapable of achieving such a tremendous task.[42]

'Abdu'l-Bahá states that consultation is 'one of the most potent instruments conducive to the tranquillity and felicity of the people.'[43] And Bahá'u'lláh attests that 'No welfare and no well-being can be attained except through consultation.'[44] Some of the most thrilling statements in the Writings tell us that this vital tool of consultation, if put to proper use, 'transmuteth conjecture into certitude', 'will always be a cause of awareness and of awakening', and manifests 'The maturity of the gift of understanding . . . .'[45]

In order to learn this extraordinary language, we are reminded by Shoghi Effendi, we must somehow succeed in holding all contraries in harmony, and the ability to achieve such a feat, through the power of consultation, is 'Nothing short of the spirit of a true Bahá'í . . .'. For it is only that spirit, speaking the language of consultation, that can hope to reconcile 'the principles of mercy and justice, of freedom and submission, of the sanctity of the right of the individual and of self-surrender, of vigilance, discretion and prudence on the one hand, and fellowship, candor, and courage on the other.'[46]

Consultation is the voice of collaboration between the individual and the community; it brings together in fresh combinations the same elements of intense commitment and detached perspective we have encountered before. It must be a language which encourages the independent candour of individual understanding, and simultaneously protects the close bonds of connection between people. It invites frankness as an obligation and prescribes tact and courtesy as a condition. It is at once the voice of intercession on behalf of an individual's rights, and at the same time voices the indispensable need for the individual to submit to its decisions.

The ability to feel free and effective in a Bahá'í community is not something to be claimed vociferously as a right. If this were so, we would encounter constant and divisive challenge and disharmony amongst ourselves, questioning, protesting, undermining and negating the authority of the Assemblies and the motives of individuals. At its most extreme, this fallacy of judgement would lead us to utter loss, the bond between us and the Covenant broken, the life-giving and mysterious throb along the spirit's arteries quite stilled. On the contrary, the rights of freedom and effective action lie with the Assemblies themselves to protect. As advocates they step in on behalf of individuals, draw upon their talents, recognize their strengths, and release them from the limitations of conformity to serve the Cause. As receptive instruments turned towards their divine source, the Assemblies are able to reflect unprejudiced opinions and unbiased justice in their decisions more faithfully than individuals can do. And thus they are the most appropriate instruments to safeguard and stimulate personal initiative.

Within the structure of the Administrative Order, moreover, we find the dual and complementary institutions of Spiritual Assemblies on the one hand and Counsellors and their Auxiliary Boards on the other. And here again we confront the vital necessity for response and receptivity between these two arms of authority and encouragement. If the equation of tongue and ear, with all its flexibility which we have previously discussed, is effective on a private and individual level of life, it is hardly surprising to find here, too, in the majestic patterns of the

Administrative Order, reflections of the greater and lesser patterns of the universe. In a society characterized by disintegration, disruption and divorce between all kinds of pairs, we find ourselves the inheritors of Bahá'u'lláh's World Order, holding in our hands the tools and instruments of consultation and collaboration that are destined to build a spiritually-oriented civilization. Indeed, we have to admit that the sundering of ties has been necessary; the disintegration had to take place. The traditional relationships between men and women, individuals and community, had to be shaken and reversed to allow Bahá'u'lláh's revitalized principles to fall into place. As Shoghi Effendi affirms,

> Such simultaneous processes of rise and of fall, of integration and of disintegration, of order and chaos, with their continuous and reciprocal reactions on each other, are but aspects of a greater Plan, one and indivisible, whose Source is God . . .[47]

But in recombining the elements of order once more, we need to guard against being reactionary, for the new bonds of connection anticipated in the Bahá'í Writings are as different from the old as light from fire and truth from denial. The mingling of contraries must characterize the actual process of consultation itself, for unless all the participants are both ear and tongue, are both the active force at one time and its recipient at another, consultation will not take place. Even as an individual teacher, at the very moment when he is offering the message to another soul, must be sensitive to the receptivity of his hearer, so too within any consultative body the 'male' and 'female' roles must be interchanged with fluid ease between us. Indeed, the process identified by Shoghi Effendi as the steps to be taken by an individual in his efforts to teach would seem to

apply also to the steps to be taken collaboratively within an institution, during the subtle interchange of
consultation:

Let him consider the degree of his hearer's receptivity . . . Let
him remember the example set by 'Abdu'l-Bahá, and His
constant admonition to shower such kindness . . ., and exemp-
lify to such a degree the spirit of the teachings . . ., that the
recipient will be spontaneously impelled to identify himself with
the Cause . . . Let him refrain . . . from insisting on such . . .
observances as might impose too severe a strain . . .[48]

During consultation, as in teaching, and indeed in any
exchange between people that intends to be more than a
parallel monologue, the receptivity of the hearer plays as
vital a role as the substance of a speech. The example of
'Abdu'l-Bahá – like His presence during a Spiritual
Assembly meeting in which true consultation is taking
place[49] – surely reminds us of the quality of our response to
each other, and instils in us the desire for that ideal communication mentioned earlier. And if, by His grace, we
are aware, with our newly-awakened powers of consultation, of our differences melting, our opposing idea
harmonizing, and our separations becoming interlinked
by bonds of oneness then we need to guard against dog-
matism of method and restriction of procedure which
might 'impose too severe a strain' on the heart's new-born
response between us. Finally, the decisions we come to
during a consultation, like the fruits of teaching the Faith,
are intended to infuse into the community and ourselves
'so deep a longing' as to impel us to arise and devote our
energies 'to the quickening of other souls'.[50]

The languages of compassion and consultation, therefore, are different and yet they are the same. Both have as

their goal the quickening of hearts, but this quickening would not take place were it not for the interaction between contraries. To commit oneself to the mysterious and life-giving process of consultation, an individual must needs create a merging within himself of the tongue and the ear, the speaker and the spoken-to. He must recognize that 'Such as communicate the generating influence and such as receive its impact are indeed created through the irresistible Word of God',[51] and, free from a rigid adherence to either one or the other role, he must submit himself to the powers of both, transmitted through that Word.

CHAPTER SEVEN

The Mother Word

The Mother Temple

From the individual lamp and the shining mansion of the
divine institutions of the Cause, we cast our eyes further up
and find the luminous architecture of the Temples, those
symbols of the Word of God amongst mankind. And it is in
the architectural metaphor of the Temples that we come
closest to the literal form of 'this glorious structure' referred to by Bahá'u'lláh in the *Tablet of Wisdom*. For in its
spiritual sense 'the real temple is the very Word of God'
and is a symbol of 'the divine uniting force'[1] at work in the
world. Like the lamp of the individual soul and the
gleaming altar of the Assemblies, the Temple is the external form whose transparency of motive and expression
enables the indwelling light of the Revelation to beam out
upon the world. 'Abdu'l-Bahá seems to be referring to
both the inner and outer temples when He writes, in a
letter to a 'lady of the Kingdom', expressing the hope that

. . . from the bounties of Bahá'u'lláh, thou mayest daily advance in the Kingdom, that thou mayest become a heavenly
angel, confirmed by the breaths of the Holy Spirit, and

mayest erect a structure that shall eternally remain firm and unshakeable . . .[2]

It would seem that the influence of the Word of God in this day is of such potency that, should we combine the penetrating influence of utterance with 'the tokens of divine wisdom which are recorded in the sacred Books and Tablets',[3] there would indeed be raised within our hearts a structure to correspond with the House of Worship. For just as we should direct our steps at the hour of dawn to the Mashriqu'l-Adhkár in order to commune with our Beloved and conform our lives to His laws, so too from the dawning moment of our understanding of this Cause, we should hear songs of praise raised from the inward temples of our hearts, and find the doors of the sacred Writings opening wide before us.

But the Mashriqu'l-Adhkár, like all other structures we have met, combines contraries. It connects the silent power of the verses of God with a wheel of social, educational and philanthropic institutions that cluster around the Temple. It symbolizes a fusion between spirit and form once more. It is a place where we 'sit in silence to hearken', and then proceed to act, speak, and implement our powers in schools, hospitals, universities, and other forms of work and service. It harmonizes the active and the receptive roles in our lives, and even the mysterious name of 'the silent Teacher' which we apply to the Temple tells us of this extraordinary merging. The profound eloquence of such a tranquil edifice, even as the quality of the lives of women like Ṭáhirih, Navváb, and the Greatest Holy Leaf, affects us without strident claims on our conscious knowledge. Like the verses of God chanted in the privacy of our chambers, the 'virtue of the grace vouchsafed' to this symbol of His Word 'must needs sooner or later exercise its influence' on the world and 'cause the heart of every righteous man to throb.'[4] Bahá'u'lláh conveys the resplendent nature of the Word of God in this age when He writes:

O My Name! The Day-Star of utterance . . . hath so illumined the Scrolls and Tablets that the kingdom of utterance and the exalted dominion of understanding vibrate with joy and ecstasy and shine forth with the splendour of His light . . .[5]

But He also acknowledges our illiteracy, adding, 'yet the generality of mankind comprehend not'.

As 'Abdu'l-Bahá confirms, 'the scales are already shifting'.[6] Force, vociferous demand, and aggressive assertion have too long blighted the world. Humanity is weary of noise, and hungers for silence. The traditional roles of dominance and subservience have so shifted that even those who rule by force must feel their impotence, and those who rise to power experience powerlessness. We have begun to recognize that our wars and ravages in the past and in the present are due to a crucial lack of balance. We have begun to express the realization voiced by 'Abdu'l-Bahá half a century ago that 'humanity has been defective and inefficient because incomplete.'[7]

The Writings concerning the eventual rise and recognition of the vital qualities inherent in women cast a compelling light on our response to the Word of God. There is no doubt that if 'the silent Teacher' and its mysterious powers are to affect our lives as thoroughly as would appear from the statements about the institution of the Mashriqu'l-Adhkár made by the Master and Shoghi Effendi, then 'the generality of mankind' must necessarily acquire capacities and qualities that we would associate with the receptive agent, the 'feminine' attributes or the Eve within each one of us. 'Abdu'l-Bahá states that while man has dominated in the past because of his more forceful and aggressive qualities,

... force is [now] losing its weight, and mental alertness, intuition, and the spiritual qualities of love and service, in which woman is strong, are gaining ascendancy. Hence the new age will be an age less masculine and more permeated with the feminine ideals, or, to speak more exactly, will be an age in which the masculine and feminine elements of civilization will be more properly balanced.[8]

But how can civilization become 'more permeated with feminine ideals' unless we begin to respond with 'a hearing ear' to the Word of God, and allow its generating influence to affect the quality of our lives? To receive the full impact and potency of God's Revelation is not a passive occupation, but one whose rigorous demands upon our creative faculties enable us to become the quickeners of mankind.[9] Surely the high station afforded to mothers in this Day has profound spiritual implications that reach beyond the specific task of raising children to the collective task of raising souls to carry forward an ever-advancing civilization.

It is clear therefore that the future generation depends on the mothers of today. Is not this vital responsibility for the woman? Does she not require every possible advantage to equip her for such a task?[10]

The Inward Eve

If we are able to recognize the 'feminine' strengths with which we have all been endowed, would not such advantages and encouragement also apply to this Eve within us?

If her capacities of spiritual susceptibility and intense commitment to bonds are not well integrated within us, but are dominated instead by the external virtues of organized activity and self-assertion, how then can we nurture and teach the souls around us, or train the children of men to grow towards an independent recognition of the Cause? The 'mother' within each one of us, deprived of recognition and responsibility, will remain ignorant, will be unable to express her powers, and will cramp, flaw and restrict the quality of all our actions:

If the mother is educated then her children will be well taught. When the mother is wise, then will the children be led into the path of wisdom. If the mother be religious she will show her children how they should love God. If the mother is moral she guides her little ones into the ways of uprightness.[11]

We have peopled the world with our ragged actions, our little savage deeds that roam unparented and barefoot through the cities' streets. Wild they were born and brutal grew, unchecked, unchastened and unclaimed by the inward Eve, who was herself unnamed and kept despised in the back streets of our sophisticated minds. And coming to maturity we find our orphans grown monstrous, vagabonds that trail the streets, marauding gangs that lie in wait to seize on friendship, beggars on the temple steps of trust. And huddled in obscurity within our souls, leaning over balconies of superstition, the mother of our acts and deeds remains degraded and deprived of self-respect.

Of course the passage from the Writings quoted above has a specific purpose: it is the tempered guidance of 'Abdu'l-Bahá for the education and advancement of women in general and mothers in particular, who are primarily responsible for the upbringing of the next generation. But the mysterious power implicit in the Sacred

Word is such that it flowers with a particular relevance for all humanity. While it is the prescribed remedy revealed by the Divine Physician for this particular age and these particular souls among an ailing humanity, it also conveys truth to every one, and does not fade in vitality and brilliance though the ages of men roll past. Within each utterance of Bahá'u'lláh and the Báb and 'Abdu'l-Bahá, therefore, we need to recognize the immediate reference as well as the eternal one: the specific relevance of this teaching for the needs of our time, and also the infinite shadows of immortality cast by these words on the pages of our lives.

So, while we understand this exhortation to relate to the role and education of women, we may also remember that it is a spiritual prescription for the soul of mankind. And the soul is neither man nor woman, for before God we stand without such sexual identities. The relevance of such words to the soul, therefore, directs our attention to a quality within us for which the attribute of sex is only metaphorical. For Shoghi Effendi tells us categorically that in the next world 'there is no sex, and no giving and taking in marriage'.[12] Those attributes of the soul which we must develop, in order to enhance what 'Abdu'l-Bahá refers to when He says 'the feminine elements of civilization', are surely qualities which, in the receptive, responsive, and reflective soul of man, draw it ever nearer to its God. It is not the outward manifestations of sexual distinction to which the Writings direct our attention, therefore, but their spiritual reality. The Manifestation of God calls upon all the capacities within us which reflect the creation of God: the pebbles in our souls and weeds that spring out of our dusty hearts are addressed by Him, and so are the leaping children of innocence within us, and the mothers who may or may not motivate their deeds for the betterment of the human race.

The Mother Temple is also a metaphorical name given by Shoghi Effendi to those first temples in any continent that are destined, in time, to inspire other temples that will be regarded as their offspring across the land. The Mashriqu'l-Adhkár, which is the architectural expression of the potent centre of our civilization, drawing us ever nearer to the Word of God, is also significantly a 'mother' in the sense that it symbolizes the capacities that lie latent and untapped by civilization, as well as the compassionate guidance that will train the children of men to achieve their fullest potential in the centuries that lie ahead.

The potentialities of this Institution, which are destined to create such a rich culture in the future, are recalled in Bahá'u'lláh's statement about the Word of God, whose external symbol is the Mashriqu'l-Adhkár:

Every single letter proceeding out of the mouth of God is indeed a mother letter, and every word uttered by Him Who is the Well Spring of Divine Revelation is a mother word, and His Tablet a Mother Tablet.[13]

It is immediately appropriate also that the Book revealed by each Manifestation of God should be called 'the Mother Book',[14] for from its laws, its prophetic injunctions and its praise of the Remembrance of God issue the letters, scrolls and tablets of a new day. Indeed, Bahá'u'lláh makes specific reference to the 'mother' quality of His own Revelation when He speaks of the establishment of justice in the world:

The fears and agitation which the revelation of this law provokes in men's hearts should indeed be likened to the cries of the suckling babe weaned from his mother's milk, if ye be of them that perceive.[15]

The importance of these 'feminine' elements within our lives is stressed in ways that enable us to recognize both the proximity to and remoteness from God; they become a standard by which we can recognize both mercy and justice. They provide us with the language of response, for Bahá'u'lláh Himself uses them as an example of the quality of both His longing and His love. Speaking of His intense anguish and suffering, His poverty and misery, He writes:

I swear by Thy might! I have wept with such a weeping that I have been unable to make mention of Thee, or to extol Thee, and cried with such a bitter cry that every mother in her bereavement was bewildered at me, and forgot her own anguish and the sighs she had uttered.[16]

It fills us with awe to discover that a mother's anguish and grief are taken as a standard by which to measure the suffering experienced by the Manifestation of God. By acknowledging this pain so exquisitely, Bahá'u'lláh not only resolves our own experiences but alerts us to the all-inclusive nature of the Word of God. For the 'mother' experience is taken not only as a criterion for the extremity of pain, but also for the climax of joy:

My remembrance of Thee, O my God, quencheth my thirst, and quieteth my heart. My soul delighteth in its communion with Thee, as the suckling child delighteth itself in the breasts of Thy mercy . . .[17]

The Maiden and the Flower

The 'feminine' attributes of the Word of God are associated with more than its fecundity and the abundance of spiritual nourishment with which it floods mankind. Even that pre-existent condition of love implied by Bahá'u'-lláh's assertion 'I loved thy creation, hence I created thee',[18] and His assurance of parental care, only begin to explore these attributes of 'femininity'.

. . . ere thou didst issue from thy mother's womb, I destined for thee two founts of gleaming milk, eyes to watch over thee, and hearts to love thee.[19]

Our relationship to this mysterious Word is not only as a child to its parent, but also as a lover to his Beloved, and the Beloved, too, is graced with attributes of such delicacy and refinement that the feminine metaphor once more supplies us with the quality of response which is most appropriate. Addressing the Spirit of Revelation, Bahá'u'-lláh speaks to an incarnation of exquisite beauty:

Step out of Thy holy chamber, O Maid of Heaven, inmate of the Exalted Paradise! Drape thyself in whatever manner pleaseth Thee in the silken Vesture of Immortality, and put on, in the name of the All-Glorious, the broidered Robe of Light. Hear, then, the sweet, the wondrous accent of the Voice that cometh from the Throne of Thy Lord, the Inaccessible, the Most High. Unveil Thy face, and manifest the beauty of the black-eyed Damsel, and suffer not the servants of God to be deprived of the light of Thy shining countenance.[20]

The inward love affair between the 'Maid' and her 'Lord' implicit in this passage tells us something of the mysterious union within the Word of God of all contraries and all polarities. In these luminous words of Bahá'u'lláh we sense a power which combines and resolves the contradictory impulses which so chequer our lives. There is a marriage here which enables us to conceive of a harmony in our own lives between the active force and its recipient. The following passage from *Gleanings* is an extraordinary integration of these twin forces and illustrates how we, even as we read, move the two wings within our souls with fluid ease, and to our own amazement find ourselves wind-born and flying past our limitations:

'Hear Me, ye mortal birds!' He begins, and with soft and compelling tones draws for us the outline of a delicate and tender beauty. 'In the Rose Garden of changeless splendour a Flower hath begun to bloom, compared to which every other flower is but a thorn, and before the brightness of Whose glory the very essence of beauty must pale and wither.' There could be no more loveliness than this, nothing more fair or radiant could exist; and we are hushed with awe, as though we trod through chambers of untouched purity. With the next breath, we hear the beating banners of desire and find ourselves out in the farthest fields of our approach, yearning to reach the place where we had thought we were: 'Arise, therefore, and, with the whole enthusiasm of your hearts, with all the eagerness of your souls, the full fervour of your will, and the concentrated efforts of your entire being, strive to attain the paradise of His presence . . .' It is almost a surprise to read the masculine pronoun here, however generic it may be, since we had been so entirely mesmerized in the previous sentence by the delicate 'feminine' nature of the Flower. But Bahá'u'lláh does not afford our rigid minds much rest, for, having employed the masculine drive of our desire to attain our goal, He immediately reminds us of the more subtle aspirations that lie still further ahead: 'and endeavour to inhale the fragrance of the incorruptible Flower, to breathe the sweet savours of holiness, and to obtain a portion of this perfume of celestial glory.' And the closer we approach, the more we lose sight of distinctions and contraries. For the Word of God is neither masculine nor feminine; it embraces all polarities. Indeed, we have to fuse the contraries within ourselves in order to attain and understand its potency, and thus: 'Whoso followeth this counsel will break his chains asunder, will taste the abandonment of enraptured love, will attain unto his heart's desire, and will surrender his soul into the hands of his Beloved.' The active and receptive roles are entirely blended in this climax; we claim our hopes and simultaneously surrender to our goal. The chains of comparison and conflict must necessarily break, and we find instead that we are everlastingly bound to our Beloved. With such a resolution of contraries, with such entire harmony between words and deeds, is it any wonder that the bird of humanity might now fly? 'Bursting through his cage, he will, even as the bird of the spirit, wing his flight to his holy and everlasting nest.'[21]

There is always a danger, in attempting to probe the significance and explore the magnitude of the creative Word of God, that we shall diminish and restrict it with words that limp and falter with their lack of creativity. Our private and naked relationship with the Beloved should not be violated or bruised by such fumbling gestures in a language that can never hope to reflect adequately the sweetness of His love. We need to bear in mind the separation that will always remain between the circling adoration of language and the innermost recess of the sanctuary of our faith. We can but circumambulate His threshold. No matter how near we may approach, there will always remain an unfathomable remoteness between where we stand on this carpet of words and metaphors, and that Centre of sanctity beyond even the candles of our certitude. Sometimes, by tokens and by signs in the

outer courts and pavilions of apprehension, we may perhaps arrive as close to the sealed chambers of His silence
and beauty as we might, striving through the labyrinths of
language. The very words we employ, taught by His
grace, with which we sing His praise, can become the veil
that interposes between us and His majesty. We can use
the living breath of consultation to part language and
draw us closer to His beauty, or we can use His metaphors
to lacerate His throat instead of dressing His raven locks.[22]
For the comb He gives us, like the Administrative Order
itself, can best reveal His beauty. In the same way, His
words adorn the truth of this Revelation and should be
combed rather than cut by the tools of the mind.

The King and the Comb

Indeed, how did we find ourselves so intimately close,
wandering in His chambers, fingering the mirror and the
comb? To utter His words is to be in danger of becoming
His lovers. Are we prepared to be caressed to life? Are we
ready for Him at any moment to enter these chambers and
claim us for His own? It is usually because of our hesitation
and our fears that we seize on the comb and hold it in a
gesture of defiance. To be caught so vulnerably, to be
touched so intimately, does not conform to our habits of
detached objectivity.

But what should we fear? Is He unknown to us that we
would hide ourselves, or is it dread of recognition that
holds us in inward trepidation? No degree of mental or
emotional preparation could have protected us from His
proximity. Even as we stand hesitant amidst the fading
petals of our own descriptions, even as we dimly sense the

perfume-tinted air, unready to meet Him, He stands watching, unobserved. Our absorption in the comb has itself almost deprived us of His presence:

Yet, notwithstanding, thou didst remain so wrapt in the veil of self, that thine eyes beheld not the beauty of the Beloved . . .[23]

Even as we touch the silken couch of His allusions, acquaint ourselves with the rich mantle of His rich embroidered words, we are neglecting 'all My bounties' and occupying ourselves with our 'idle imaginings, in such wise that thou didst become wholly forgetful, and, turning away from the portals of the Friend didst abide within the courts of My enemy.'[24] Tracing our fingers in awe along the crusted jewels of the new-discovered sheath which was a token of His love for us, a gift from His hand, we ignore the silent powers within. Lost in admiration of the wine cup at His table, we convey it to our lips but have not yet allowed the wine to enter us. We are surrounded by Him everywhere, and all about us lie the evidences of His wealth, His power, His love – yet the world is like a woman who keeps demanding more favours as proof of love, forgets all she has, and seems rarely to remember that 'If thou lovest Me not, My love can in no wise reach thee.'[25]

The Word, which in this relationship is the world's Lover-husband and her Lord, waits at the door for her to wake, a beauty clasped in self-forgetful sleep, or hovers with benediction round her bed, while she has made herself the prostitute of lesser pleasures. Thus the equation slips our grasp so that our souls remain perturbed and, by the very vastness of His sphere of love, our linear minds are hindered as we mention Him: 'For minds cannot grasp Me nor hearts contain Me.'[26]

However we approach the Word of God, therefore, we

discover ourselves in fresh and paradoxical relationships to it. We are forced to take stock of contraries that are resolved in it. We discover by that resolution that we can contain some measure of the harmony within ourselves. Sometimes a single word released by Him can generate 'all the manifold arts which the hands of man can produce'.[27] Yet that same 'masculine' force can also be the procreator of our deeds, mothering a thousand meanings in our lives:

No sooner is this resplendent word uttered, than its animating energies . . . give birth to the means and instruments whereby such arts can be produced and perfected.[28]

But wherever we find ourselves in the equation, whichever side of the sword we fall, we shall only understand these luminous words to the degree we permit ourselves to respond. Neither the will to act nor the capacity to receive can occupy a passive role in the affinity between the soul and the Word of God. Both are motivated by the same impulse. Whether we yearn towards Him or He hovers waiting for us to wake to His presence, whether it is father or mother that He supplies us, and whether it is as parent or lover that we recognize Him, the story of the Covenant demands that we participate. Even on the couch of heedlessness where we repose in abdication of our destiny, we still participate, and in our sullenness reap centuries of sorrow. With our capacities still unborn we linger wonderstruck in the womb of change, charged with the task of growing and of strengthening the spiritual qualities we hardly know we own, embraced by His protection, directed by the flow of His unbidden energies, and drawing ever nearer to the great limb-quaking hour when we shall be thrust against the breaking wreckage of a world that lies gasping with relief at what is born.

Thus Far and No Farther

Bahá'u'lláh tells us that if we beheld 'immortal sovereignty', we would 'strive to pass from this fleeting world',[29] transcend the limitations of its perceptions, and recognize a oneness in the divergent and contrary forces at work within it. This fleeting world has been revealed to us; immortal sovereignty has been concealed. And the journey it takes to comprehend why this is so is itself a journey towards purity of heart. The language of resolution, it would seem, cannot be altogether spelled out. Even Ṭáhirih, the unveiled, spoke from behind the curtain to communicate to the divines. Although she blazed in eloquence before the tents of Badasht, she attained the high station of martyrdom by submitting that eloquence to the white scarf of His Will. Although the spiritual strength of the Greatest Holy Leaf is surely written 'in clear characters . . . openly manifest in the holy Presence',[30] yet on this earthly plane, where things contrary to her ease and tranquillity were ordained, her station was revealed by her mute response to the Faith rather than by the implementation of her own powers.

We are also well aware that, were it not for the protective arms of silence, our failures to respond adequately to the Word of God would expose us to such shame that our capacity to respond would itself dissolve. By the infinite grace of God, our betrayals are 'breathed . . . not in My retreats above unto the hosts of holiness',[31] and the Divine Spirit, while weeping at our rejection, has 'concealed thy secret and desired not thy shame'.[32] Indeed there are mysteries in the fact of concealment that tell as much as that which we have heard:

All that I have revealed unto thee with the tongue of power, and have written for thee with the pen of might, hath been in accordance with thy capacity and understanding, not with My state and the melody of My voice.[33]

Bahá'u'lláh has not only opened doors for us in this Revelation, but also opened our eyes to the existence of doors beyond which we may not see. We find ourselves not only drawn to soar into His immensity, but enabled simultaneously to realize that His immensity stretches beyond our soaring. We experience the paradox, therefore, of yearning to soar above our limitations, while realizing that we can 'in no wise . . . transcend the limitations which a contingent world hath imposed . . .'[34] Bahá'u'lláh warns us: 'O Son of Man! Transgress not thy limits, nor claim that which beseemeth thee not.'[35] Indeed our limits of time and space, and all the contraries we have previously alluded to, constitute the very means by which we can arrive at the station of submission.

When we explore these limits, and touch the threaded links – the enigmas and interrelationships between us and within us – we are dazzled by the star-dust in ourselves, and vibrate with the complementary harmonies we find. Thus we can reach the quiet command, 'Question it not, nor have a doubt thereof,'[36] and can obey because we have at last learned to admit, knowing our limitations, our powerlessness to judge when it is that our doubts have been answered. Such submission, therefore, implied by the injunction 'Thus far and no farther', ushers us into a fresh world of discovery and growth, for the seeds of wisdom and knowledge, hidden in the language of concealment, can rise green and tender from the soil of humility and receptivity associated with the heart.

Wherefore sow the seeds of wisdom and knowledge in the pure soil of the heart, and keep them hidden, till the hyacinths of divine wisdom spring from the heart and not from mire and clay.[37]

Bearing with us a faint memory of that incorruptible Flower, we find at last the fragrance of the hidden hyacinths within our hearts, rising with a quiet vitality that reminds us of the lives of others, more calm, more vivid, more intensely perfumed than our own. Here grow the blossoms of spiritual beauty that have through the winter long remained concealed from our external eyes; they can only lift their myriad petals towards the generating energies of the Word of God in a gentle and responsive breeze; they can only rise to fragrance if they yearn to convey their bloom to others; they can only find nourishment of wisdom and knowledge in a condition of humility and servitude symbolized by the dust beneath our feet. For the language of the hyacinths is a silent one; they speak in fragrance and must be nourished to be heard. Had they sprung from mire and clay, the seeds that had for such long latent years remained hidden would not have flowered with divine wisdom. And so the metaphorical seeds planted by Bahá'u'lláh in His Writings, like the seeds of meaning scattered by the hand of God throughout creation, need to take root in the purity of our response and not in a limiting world of conflict and contention.

So too, like seeds, like certitude and all growing things, we find the language of the soul brings us full circle to the tug and pull of contraries that lead us to our goal. But now, as we experience the joyous swing of these God-graced polarities within us, we perceive amazed that all the time we thought the hidden language lay beyond our grasp, and had to be explored with pickaxe and with power of tongue, it lay quite still within. We are the language that we would have learned. We are the hidden voice that yet might sing. We are the poem and the song, and having heard the Tongue of Grandeur, we can wing our way to be the echo of His words.

Now amidst all the peoples of the world must the beloved arise, with a heart even as the day-star, a strong inward urge, a shining brow, a musk-scented breath, a tongue speaking ever of God, an exposition crystal-clear . . . let them be verses of perfection on the page of the universe' . . . 'the letters inscribed upon His sacred scroll' . . . 'potent signs, resplendent standards, and perfect as Thy Word.[38]

Conclusion

WE HAVE been driving to the frontiers of permission, and
have found that 'minds cannot grasp Me nor hearts contain Me'.[1] We have stood at the border between the voice
in our own veins and the call from beyond us that summons to eternity. And we responded. But even at that
moment, we became aware of a returning in us. We knew
that although we searched the universe for evermore, our
quest would be in vain. Even as we leapt towards eternity,
we knew that our quest was all we could perceive of it, and
so to leap towards the call we heard was all we could
achieve, again and again.

The farmer, who could only know the secrets of the sky
in basketfuls and taste heaven only in a single maiden, had
no knowledge of the limitation of his vision. He had not
learnt about the relativity of truth as he perceived it, and
mistakenly measured the sky by what he could see in a
straw basket. The vast azure overhead and the empty air
in the basket were the same in kind, but, unaware of the
limited receptacle of his own mind, he judged the mysteries of creation by the cramped perceptions immediately
available to him. His motives for peeping into the basket
were grounded upon the sharp distinctions of his limited
perceptions too. He had no goal, no insatiable desire to
learn about the sky, but only a certain curiosity about his

bride. For he had also divided himself into basketfuls: he had married the maiden only in a material sense, and had not recognized her to be the spiritual aspects of himself. So long as that deep divorce would separate him, and the white rope of the Covenant remain inaccessible to him, he would be an exile of the sky, deprived of marriage and maiden, wandering in the pastures of this world.

Yet even if we should learn the language of the soul and cling to the white rope of the Word of God, we could not enter into places where a farmer may not go. Although a glimpse of what lies couched and waiting in the meadows of the sky might send us fleet past all need for cows, yet so long as we are living we are farmers, and remain on this contingent plane. We cannot transcend our limitations, but we can integrate our powers. The milk of our material means can nourish the maidens of our spiritual civilization. We can recognize the bond between our baskets and the unbounded blue above us, and link ourselves in love and humility instead of ignorance and need.

To recognize the oneness within ourselves and around us in this fragmented world is the goal of every soul. To respond to the interlinking universe with the softly singing cells of our beings is the craving that keeps us alive. To bear witness to the oneness and communicate the response in deeds and words and wonder give purpose to the life of a Bahá'í.

Progressive revelation teaches us that response must be sustained by constant repetition. At the simplest level of our lives we know this to be true. Bonds need replenishment, and strengthening and renewal; responsiveness cannot survive a dearth of return. The subtle interrelationships between people need to be reaffirmed repeatedly and nourished by echoes of confirmation, or they will wither away and die. Within individual friendships and the inter-flow of guidance and inspiration between the institutions of the Cause, this same need for repeated response can be found. For nothing, it seems, in this marvellous creation can happen only in one form and at one time. Variations of expression and reconciliation abound, and while a single gesture is unique and cannot be repeated, the principle must be at work again and again for the gesture to develop into a dance, for the motion to flood into full flight, for the single syllables of our perceptions and efforts to blend into words and sentences and tell of the glory of God.

And so the circle is complete, for, having once responded, we know of nothing sweeter, and yearn to repeat the gesture and discover ourselves again replenished by it. We come back to the beginning of our insatiable desire to leap the page, to seize the rope and climb, to find a language that will convey light upon light with both vision and form. And the books lie open, waiting for us to read and discover ourselves to be this very language. Revelation and creation are calling upon us to respond to the ringing truth of this mighty Cause. The Blessed Beauty has summoned us with a clear message. And what appeal, Shoghi Effendi asks us, could be more direct and more moving than these 'most touching, most inspiring words' of 'Abdu'l-Bahá:

O how I long to see the loved ones taking upon themselves the responsibilities of the Cause! . . . I am straining my ears toward the East and toward the West, toward the North and toward the South that haply I may hear the songs of love and fellowship chanted in the meetings of the faithful . . .

The mystic Nightingale is warbling for them all; will they not listen? The Bird of Paradise is singing; will they not heed? The

Angel of Abhá is calling to them; will they not hearken? The Herald of the Covenant is pleading; will they not obey?

Ah me, I am waiting, waiting, to hear the joyful tidings . . . Will they not gladden my heart? Will they not satisfy my yearning? Will they not manifest my wish? Will they not fulfil my heart's desire? Will they not give ear to my call?[2]

Bibliography

'Abdu'l-Bahá. *Paris Talks*. London: Bahá'í Publishing Trust, 11th edn 1969. (Published by Bahá'í Publishing Trust, Wilmette, Illinois, under the title *The Wisdom of 'Abdu'l-Bahá*.)

——*The Promulgation of Universal Peace*. Chicago: Vol. I, Bahai Temple Unity, 1922; Vol. II, Bahá'í Publishing Committee, 1925.

——*Selections from the Writings of 'Abdu'l-Bahá*. Compiled by the Research Department of the Universal House of Justice; translated by a Committee at the Bahá'í World Centre and by Marzieh Gail. Haifa: Bahá'í World Centre, 1978.

Báb, The *Selections from the Writings of the Báb*. Compiled by the Research Department of the Universal House of Justice and translated by Habib Taherzadeh with the assistance of a Committee at the Bahá'í World Centre. Haifa: Bahá'í World Centre, 1976.

Bahá'í Holy Places at the World Centre. Haifa: Bahá'í World Centre, 1968.

Bahá'í Prayers. A Selection. London: Bahá'í Publishing Trust, rev. edn 1975.

Bahá'í World, The. Vol. V 1932–1934. New York: Bahá'í Publishing Committee, 1936.

Bahá'u'lláh. *Epistle to the Son of the Wolf*. Translated by Shoghi Effendi. Wilmette, Illinois: Bahá'í Publishing Trust, rev. edn 1976.

——*Gleanings from the Writings of Bahá'u'lláh*. Translated by Shoghi Effendi. Wilmette, Illinois: Bahá'í Publishing Trust, 2nd rev. edn 1976. London: Bahá'í Publishing Trust, rev. edn 1978.

——*The Hidden Words*. Translated by Shoghi Effendi. London: Bahá'í Publishing Trust. 1949. Wilmette, Illinois: Bahá'í Publishing Trust, rev. edn 1954.

——*Prayers and Meditations by Bahá'u'lláh*. Translated by Shoghi Effendi. Wilmette, Illinois: Bahá'í Publishing Trust, 6th RP 1974; London: Bahá'í Publishing Trust, rev. edn 1978.

——*The Proclamation of Bahá'u'lláh to the kings and leaders of the world*. Haifa: Bahá'í World Centre, 1967.

Tablets of Bahá'u'lláh. Compiled by the Research Department of the Universal House of Justice and translated by Habib Taherzadeh with the assistance of a Committee at the Bahá'í World Centre. Haifa: Bahá'í World Centre, 1978.

The Divine Art of Living. Selection from the Writings of Bahá'u'lláh and 'Abdu'l-Bahá. Compiled by Mabel Hyde Paine. Wilmette, Illinois: Bahá'í Publishing Trust, 4th rev. edn 1979.

The Gift of Teaching. Extracts from the Writings of Bahá'u'lláh, 'Abdu'l-Bahá, and Shoghi Effendi. Compilation issued by the Universal House of Justice. London: Bahá'í Publishing Trust, no. 9 of series, 1977.

The Heaven of Divine Wisdom. Details as for title above; no. 10 of series, 1978.

Local Spiritual Assemblies. Details as for second title above; no. 1 of series, 1970.

Miller, Jean Baker. *Toward a New Psychology of Women.* Boston: Beacon Press, 1977.

Reality of Man, The. Excerpts from Writings of Bahá'u'lláh and 'Abdu'l-Bahá. Wilmette, Illinois: Bahá'í Publishing Trust, RP 1979.

Selections from Bahá'í Scripture. Compiled and edited by David Hofman. London: Bahá'í Publishing Trust, 1941.

Shoghi Effendi. *The Advent of Divine Justice.* Wilmette, Illinois: Bahá'í Publishing Trust, rev. edn 1963.

——*Bahá'í Administration.* Wilmette, Illinois: Bahá'í Publishing Trust, rev. edn 1974.

——*God Passes By.* Wilmette, Illinois: Bahá'í Publishing Trust, 7th RP 1974.

——*Messages to the Bahá'í World.* 1950–1957. Wilmette, Illinois: Bahá'í Publishing Trust, 1971.

——with Sitarih Khanum (Lady Blomfield). *The Passing of 'Abdu'l-Bahá.* London. Bahá'í Publishing Trust, undated.

——*The Promised Day Is Come.* Wilmette, Illinois: Bahá'í Publishing Trust, rev. edn 1980.

——*The World Order of Bahá'u'lláh.* Wilmette, Illinois: Bahá'í Publishing Trust, 2nd rev. edn 1974.

Star of the West. The Baha'i Magazine. Vol. IX. 1918–1919. Chicago: Bahá'í News Service. Reprinted in *Star of the West.* Vol. 5. Oxford: George Ronald, 1978.

Synopsis and Codification of the Laws and Ordinances of the Kitáb-i-Aqdas. Haifa: Bahá'í World Centre, 1973.

References

ONE: THE HIDDEN AND THE MANIFEST

1 Bahá'u'lláh, *The Hidden Words*, no. 16 (Persian).
2 ibid. no. 19 (Persian).
3 ibid. no. 21 (Persian).
4 Bahá'u'lláh, *Prayers and Meditations*, no. 39.
5 ibid. no. 40.
6 ibid. no. 69.
7 ibid. no. 68.
8 ibid. no. 40.
9 Bahá'u'lláh, *Gleanings*, p. 143 (Brit.), p. 144 (US).
10 ibid. section LXXIII.
11 'Abdu'l-Bahá, *Selections from the Writings*, p. 192.
12 Bahá'u'lláh, *Tablets of Bahá'u'lláh*, pp. 60–61.
13 'Abdu'l-Bahá, *Makátíb* (Tablets of 'Abdu'l-Bahá), Vol. I. pp. 436–7.
14 'Abdu'l-Bahá, *Selections from the Writings*, p. 198.
15 Bahá'u'lláh, *Tablets of Bahá'u'lláh*, p.60.
16 ibid. p. 141.
17 'Abdu'l-Bahá, *Makátíb*, op. cit.
18 Bahá'u'lláh, *The Hidden Words*, no. 5 (Arabic).
19 Bahá'u'lláh, *Prayers and Meditations*, no. 93.
20 Bahá'u'lláh, *Gleanings*, p. 266 (Brit.), p. 267 (US).
21 *A Synopsis and Codification of the Kitáb-i-Aqdas*, p. 16.
22 Bahá'u'lláh, *The Hidden Words*, no. 36 (Persian).
23 'Abdu'l-Bahá, *Selections from the Writings*, p. 119.
24 Bahá'u'lláh, *Tablets of Bahá'u'lláh*, p. 140.
25 ibid.
26 Bahá'u'lláh, *The Hidden Words*, no. 66 (Arabic).

TWO: THE HEARING EAR

1 Bahá'u'lláh, *Tablets of Bahá'u'lláh*, p. 172.
2 ibid.
3 ibid. p. 62.

4 ibid. p. 173.

5 ibid.

6 Bahá'u'lláh, *The Hidden Words*, no. 77 (Persian).

7 Shoghi Effendi, *The Promised Day Is Come*, pp. 6–7.

8 Bahá'u'lláh, *Gleanings*, pp. 144–5 (Brit.), p. 145 (US).

9 Bahá'u'lláh, *Prayers and Meditations*, for words quoted in this paragraph: p. 212 (Brit.), p. 278 (US); p. 236 (Brit.), p. 308 (US); no. 115; no. 145.

10 Bahá'u'lláh, *The Hidden Words*, nos. 28, 30 (Persian).

11 'Abdu'l-Bahá, *Selections from the Writings*, p. 122.

12 Bahá'u'lláh, *The Hidden Words*, no. 28 (Persian).

13 Shoghi Effendi, *God Passes By*, p. 119.

14 ibid.

15 ibid. pp. 119–20.

16 ibid. p. 126.

17 Bahá'u'lláh, *Prayers and Meditations*, p. 235 (Brit.), pp. 306–7 (US).

18 ibid. p. 207 (Brit.), pp. 271–2 (US)

19 'Abdu'l-Bahá, *Selections from the Writings*, p. 216.

20 ibid. p. 222.

21 ibid. p. 119

22 *Bahá'í Holy Places*, p. 65.

23 ibid.

24 ibid. p. 66.

25 Báb, The, *Selections from the Writings*, p. 77.

26 *Bahá'í Holy Places*, pp. 65–6.

27 ibid. p. 65.

28 *Bahá'í World, The*, Vol. V, p. 169.

29 Bahá'u'lláh, *Tablets of Bahá'u'lláh*, p. 140.

30 See *Má'idiy-i-Ásmání*, Vol. I, pp. 16–17. (Compiled from Bahá'í Writings by 'Abdu'l-Ḥamíd Ishráq-Khávarí.)

31 'Abdu'l-Bahá, *Selections from the Writings*, p. 173.

32 ibid., p. 172.

33 *Bahá'í World, The*, Vol. V, words quoted in this paragraph from pp. 179, 174, 179, in that order.

THREE: ADVOCACY

1 'Abdu'l-Bahá, *Selections from the Writings*, p. 149.

2 Shoghi Effendi, *The Advent of Divine Justice*, p. 60.

3 Bahá'u'lláh, *Tablets of Bahá'u'lláh*, pp. 172–3.
4 Bahá'u'lláh, *Gleanings*, section LIII.
5 Bahá'u'lláh, *Prayers and Meditations*, no. 110.
6 ibid. no. 83.
7 ibid.
8 ibid. no. 94.
9 ibid.
10 ibid.
11 'Abdu'l-Bahá, *Selections from the Writings*, p. 115.
12 *Bahá'í World, The*, Vol. V, pp. 171–2.
13 *Bahá'í Holy Places*, pp. 69–70.
14 ibid. p. 68.
15 ibid. p. 70.
16 Shoghi Effendi, *The World Order of Bahá'u'lláh*, p. 86.
17 ibid.
18 'Abdu'l-Bahá, *Selections from the Writings*, p. 231.
19 *Bahá'í Prayers* (British), no. 64.
20 Bahá'u'lláh, *Tablets of Bahá'u'lláh*, p. 83.
21 Bahá'u'lláh, *Gleanings*, section LV.
22 ibid.
23 ibid.
24 Shoghi Effendi, *God Passes By*, p. 108.
25 *Bahá'í Holy Places*, p. 76.
26 ibid.
27 'Abdu'l-Bahá, *Selections from the Writings*, p. 236.
28 ibid. p. 76.
29 ibid. p. 161.
30 *Bahá'í Holy Places*, pp. 76–7.

FOUR: THE POWER OF UTTERANCE

1 Bahá'u'lláh, *The Hidden Words*, no. 76 (Persian).
2 'Abdu'l-Bahá, from an unpublished compilation of the Universal House of Justice concerning *The Hidden Words*, p. 3.
3 Bahá'u'lláh, *Gleanings*, p. 264 (Brit.), p. 265 (US).
4 Bahá'u'lláh, *Tablets of Bahá'u'lláh*, p. 156.
5 ibid.
6 Bahá'u'lláh, *The Hidden Words*, no. 66 (Persian).
7 Bahá'u'lláh, *Prayers and Meditations*, no. 102.

8 Bahá'u'lláh, *Tablets of Bahá'u'lláh*, p. 172.
9 Miller, *Towards a New Psychology of Women*, p. 116.
10 Bahá'u'lláh, *Epistle to the Son of the Wolf*, p. 55.
11 Báb, The, *Selections from the Writings*, p. 77.
12 'Abdu'l-Bahá, *Paris Talks*, p. 163.
13 'Abdu'l-Bahá, *Promulgation of Universal Peace*, Vol. II, p. 277.
14 'Abdu'l-Bahá, *Paris Talks*, p. 163.
15 ibid. p. 133.
16 Bahá'u'lláh, *Tablets of Bahá'u'lláh*, p. 172.
17 ibid.
18 Bahá'u'lláh, *The Hidden Words*, no. 5 (Persian).
19 ibid. no. 72 (Persian).
20 Bahá'u'lláh, *Gleanings*, p. 158 (Brit.), p. 159 (US).
21 Shoghi Effendi, *God Passes By*, for words quoted in this paragraph: pp. 33, 31, 32.
22 ibid. pp. 32–3.
23 ibid. p. 32.
24 Bahá'u'lláh, *Tablets of Bahá'u'lláh*, p. 140.
25 Bahá'u'lláh, *The Proclamation of Bahá'u'lláh*, p. 105.
26 Bahá'u'lláh, *Tablets of Bahá'u'lláh*, p. 254.
27 'Abdu'l-Bahá, *Selections from the Writings*, p. 123.
28 Shoghi Effendi, *The Advent of Divine Justice*, p. 39.

FIVE: BONDS

1 Bahá'u'lláh, *Tablets of Bahá'u'lláh*, p. 163.
2 Quoted in 'Abdu'l-Bahá, *Selections from the Writings*, p. 119.
3 ibid. p. 63.
4 ibid.
5 'Abdu'l-Bahá in *The Reality of Man*, p. 32.
6 ibid.
7 ibid.
8 'Abdu'l-Bahá, *Promulgation of Universal Peace*, Vol., I, p. 73.
9 Bahá'u'lláh, *The Hidden Words*, no. 21 (Persian).
10 Shoghi Effendi in *Bahá'í News* (American), no. 123, p. 2.
11 'Abdu'l-Bahá, *Promulgation of Universal Peace*, Vol. I, p. 73.
12 Bahá'u'lláh, *The Hidden Words*, no. 20 (Persian).
13 Bahá'u'lláh, *Gleanings*, section V.
14 ibid.

15 ibid.
16 'Abdu'l-Bahá in *Má'idiy-i-Ásmání*, Vol. II, p. 102. (Compiled from Bahá'í Writings by 'Abdu'l-Ḥamíd Isḥráq-Khávarí.)
17 'Abdu'l-Bahá, *Promulgation of Universal Peace*, Vol. I, p. 73.
18 'Abdu'l-Bahá, *Selections from the Writings*, p. 99.
19 'Abdu'l-Bahá, *Promulgation of Universal Peace*, Vol. I, p. 170.
20 'Abdu'l-Bahá, *Paris Talks*, p. 184.
21 *Selections from Bahá'í Scripture*, p. 191.
22 Bahá'u'lláh, *The Hidden Words*, no. 2 (Arabic).
23 'Abdu'l-Bahá, *Selections from the Writings*, p. 72.
24 ibid. p. 73.
25 ibid. p. 236.
26 Bahá'u'lláh, *The Hidden Words*, no. 19 (Persian).
27 ibid. no. 36 (Arabic).
28 Bahá'u'lláh, *Gleanings*, section CV.
29 *A Synopsis and Codificaton of the Kitáb-i-Aqdas*, p. 15, no. 7.
30 ibid.
31 'Abdu'l-Bahá, *Selections from the Writings*, p. 297.
32 *Bahá'í World, The*, Vol. V, p. 179.
33 Shoghi Effendi, *God Passes By*, p. 32.
34 'Abdu'l-Bahá, *Selections from the Writings*, p. 89.
35 ibid. pp. 117–18.
36 ibid. p. 95.
37 ibid. p. 102.
38 ibid. p. 114.
39 ibid. p. 90.
40 ibid. p. 198.
41 Bahá'u'lláh, *Tablets of Bahá'u'lláh*, pp. 142–3.
42 ibid. p. 142.
43 ibid. p. 140.
44 ibid. p. 168.
45 Shoghi Effendi, *The Advent of Divine Justice*, p. 2.
46 Bahá'u'lláh, *Tablets of Bahá'u'lláh*, p. 143.
47 Shoghi Effendi, *God Passes By*, p. 325.
48 ibid.

SIX: COMPASSION AND CONSULTATION

1 'Abdu'l-Bahá, *Selections from the Writings*, p. 157.

2 ibid.
3 ibid.
4 ibid.
5 Shoghi Effendi, *The World Order of Bahá'u'lláh*, p. 42.
6 'Abdu'l-Bahá, *Selections from the Writings*, p. 157.
7 Bahá'u'lláh, *The Hidden Words*, no. 1 (Arabic).
8 Bahá'u'lláh, *Tablets of Bahá'u'lláh*, p. 142.
9 ibid. p. 143.
10 From a letter written on behalf of Shoghi Effendi, 5 October 1950, in *Bahá'í News* (American), no. 241, p. 2.
11 Bahá'u'lláh, *Tablets of Bahá'u'lláh*: the 'twin luminaries' and words quoted in this paragraph will be found in pp. 168–71.
12 'Abdu'l-Bahá, *Selections from the Writings*, p. 119.
13 Bahá'u'lláh, *Gleanings*, section CXXVI.
14 Bahá'u'lláh, *The Hidden Words*, no. 11 (Arabic).
15 ibid. no. 14 (Arabic).
16 ibid. no. 33 (Arabic).
17 ibid. no. 20 (Arabic).
18 ibid. no. 69 (Persian).
19 *Divine Art of Living, The*, p. 62.
20 Bahá'u'lláh, *Gleanings*, p. 294 (Brit.), p. 295 (US).
21 Bahá'u'lláh, *The Hidden Words*, no. 19 (Persian).
22 'Abdu'l-Bahá, *Selections from the Writings*, p. 108.
23 ibid.
24 *The Gift of Teaching*, p. 7.
25 Báb, The, *Selections from the Writings*, p. 77.
26 Bahá'u'lláh, *Tablets of Bahá'u'lláh*, p. 143.
27 See Shoghi Effendi, *The Advent of Divine Justice*, p. 42, for words of Bahá'u'lláh quoted in this sentence.
28 *Bahá'í Prayers* (British), no. 22.
29 Bahá'u'lláh, *The Hidden Words*, no. 8 (Persian).
30 Bahá'u'lláh, *Tablets of Bahá'u'lláh*, p. 143.
31 Bahá'u'lláh, *Prayers and Meditations*, p. 205 (Brit.), p. 269 (US).
32 ibid. p. 205 (Brit.), pp. 269–70 (US).
33 ibid. p. 216 (Brit.), p. 283 (US).
34 Bahá'u'lláh, *The Hidden Words*, no. 32 (Persian).
35 ibid.
36 ibid. no. 69 (Persian).

37 ibid. no. 23 (Persian).
38 ibid. no. 57 (Persian).
39 ibid. no. 71 (Arabic).
40 ibid. no. 73 (Persian).
41 Shoghi Effendi, *Messages to the Bahá'í World*, pp. 54–5.
42 *The Heaven of Divine Wisdom*, p. 11.
43 ibid. p. 7.
44 ibid. p. 3.
45 ibid.
46 Shoghi Effendi, *Principles of Bahá'í Administration*, p. 44.
47 Shoghi Effendi, *The Advent of Divine Justice*, p. 61.
48 ibid. p. 43.
49 *Local Spiritual Assemblies*, p. 3, and *The Heaven of Divine Wisdom*, p. 8.
50 Shoghi Effendi, *The Advent of Divine Justice*, p. 43.
51 Bahá'u'lláh, *Tablets of Bahá'u'lláh*, p. 140.

SEVEN: THE MOTHER WORD

1 'Abdu'l-Bahá, *Promulgation of Universal Peace*, Vol. I, p. 62.
2 'Abdu'l-Bahá, *Selections from the Writings*, p. 199.
3 'Abdu'l-Bahá, *Tablets of Bahá'u'lláh*, p. 199.
4 Bahá'u'lláh, *Gleanings*, p. 294 (Brit.), p. 295 (US).
5 Bahá'u'lláh, *Tablets of Bahá'u'lláh*, p. 199.
6 *Star of the West*, Vol. IX, no. 7, p. 87.
7 'Abdu'l-Bahá, *Promulgation of Universal Peace*, Vol. I, p. 104.
8 *Star of the West*, supra.
9 Bahá'u'lláh, *Tablets of Bahá'u'lláh*, p. 199.
10 'Abdu'l-Bahá, *Paris Talks*, p. 162.
11 ibid.
12 Extract from an unpublished letter written on behalf of Shoghi Effendi to an individual, 4 December 1954.
13 Bahá'u'lláh, *Gleanings*, section LXXIV.
14 The 'Mother Book' is frequently mentioned by Bahá'u'lláh and the Báb; see, for example, *Tablets of Bahá'u'lláh*, pp. 21, 48, 74, 247, and *Selections from the Writings of the Báb*, pp. 45, 58, 71.
15 Bahá'u'lláh, *Gleanings*, section LXXXVIII.
16 Bahá'u'lláh, *Prayers and Meditations*, p. 207 (Brit.), p. 271 (US).
17 ibid. p. 149 (Brit.), p. 195 (US).
18 Bahá'u'lláh, *The Hidden Words*, no. 4 (Arabic).

19 ibid. no. 29 (Persian).
20 Bahá'u'lláh, *Gleanings*, pp. 281–2 (Brit.), pp. 282–3 (US).
21 ibid. pp. 319–20 (Brit.), pp. 320–21 (US).
22 Bahá'u'lláh, *The Hidden Words*, no. 79 (Persian).
23 ibid. no. 22 (Persian).
24 ibid. no. 29 (Persian).
25 ibid. no. 5 (Arabic).
26 ibid. no. 66 (Arabic).
27 Bahá'u'lláh, *Gleanings*, section LXXIV.
28 ibid.
29 Bahá'u'lláh, *The Hidden Words*, no. 41 (Persian).
30 ibid. no. 59 (Persian).
31 ibid. no. 28 (Persian).
32 ibid. no. 27 (Persian).
33 ibid. no. 67 (Arabic).
34 Bahá'u'lláh, *Prayers and Meditations*, p. 67 (Brit.), p. 88 (US).
35 Bahá'u'lláh, *The Hidden Words*, no. 24 (Arabic).
36 ibid. no. 12 (Arabic).
37 ibid. no. 36 (Persian).
38 This passage is taken from the following sources: *Selections from the Writings of 'Abdu'l-Bahá*, p. 232; Shoghi Effendi, *The Advent of Divine Justice*, p. 63; *Bahá'í Prayers* (British), p. 98.

CONCLUSION

1 Bahá'u'lláh, *The Hidden Words*, no. 66 (Arabic).
2 *The Passing of 'Abdu'l-Bahá*, p. 27–8.